Elderescence

The Gift of Longevity

Jane Thayer
Peggy Thayer

Hamilton Books
an imprint of
The Rowman & Littlefield Publishing Group
Lanham • Boulder • New York • Toronto • Oxford

Copyright © 2005 by
Hamilton Books
4501 Forbes Boulevard
Suite 200
Lanham, Maryland 20706
UPA Acquisitions Department (301) 459-3366

PO Box 317
Oxford
OX2 9RU, UK

Library of Congress Control Number: 2005921631
ISBN 0-7618-3145-2 (clothbound : alk. ppr.)
ISBN 0-7618-3146-0 (paperback : alk. ppr.)

We dedicate our book to G. Stanley Hall, the trailblazer who, nearly a century ago, first identified the post-retirement period. He is often affectionately and with genuine admiration called 'the father of psychology,' or 'the kingmaker.' With his two-volume book *Adolescence* (1904), Hall gave prominence to the teenage life stage. In S*enescence* (1922), published two years after he retired and two years before his death at age eighty-one, he identified and described the last half of life. With great candor he gave an honest depiction of his own experience of retirement, which he likened to *being put out to pasture*.

Hall foresaw the emergence of a new stage of life, which we have called *elderescence*. In his own words:

> *For the hope of mankind—look for the salvation in the prolongation of human life that man may have a longer apprenticeship he now needs in order to wisely direct the ever more complex affairs of civilization, ultimately obliterating all national boundaries and racial prejudices and organizing a world state, a parliament of man, a federation of the world. The human race is at a dangerous age. There is only too much to indicate that mankind, in Europe at least if not throughout the world, has reached the 'dangerous age' that marks the dawn of senescence and that, unless we can develop what Renan calls a 'new social consciousness', and a new instinct for service and for posterity, our elaborate civilization with its institutions will surely become a Frankenstein monster . . .*

> *Progressive eugenics, radical and world-wide reeducation, and the development of a richer, riper old age, are our only sources of hope for we can look to no others to arrest the degenerative processes of national and individual egoism. At any rate, we have to face a new problem, namely, what is the old age of the world to be and how can we best prepare for it betimes?*

> *Ripe old age has been a slow, late, precarious, but precious acquisition of the race, perhaps not only its latest but also its highest product. Its modern representatives are pioneers . . . It certainly should go along with the corresponding prolongation of youth and increasing docility in the rising generation if we are right in charging ourselves with the duty of building a new story to the structure of human life*

Contents

Notes from the Authors

This book had its beginning with a mother and daughter sharing their fantasies. One spring day shortly after Jane (the mother) had "closed the doors" to her private psychotherapy practice, moving to live full time on Martha's Vineyard, and Peg (the daughter) had completed her doctoral studies in East-West psychology, the adventure began. Peg had used an experiential method developed by Dr. James Kidd in her dissertation entitled *The Experience of Being Creative as a Spiritual Practice.* Finding it a valuable tool, she was intrigued to test her beliefs.

As the casual talk between mother and daughter continued that afternoon, Peg expressed an interest in a collaborative effort using this experiential method as a way to understand the retirement experience. Jane's first thought was "Retirement . . . oh. I'm not interested in studying retirement . . .(a long pause) . . . but it would be great to do some research with my daughter."

Thus began an eight-year-long interplay of our thoughts and efforts to understand the experience of retirement, and the discovery of a new stage of life. Peg described to her mother the experiential method that would identify the core issues of the retirement experience. Spontaneous responses to the question, "Describe your experience of being retired," would be collected from volunteer participants. (The method is described in the Appendices). We sought volunteers from the Vineyard community, the American Psychological Association's file of recent retirees, retirees from the Federal government, the Massachusetts Psychological Association, from published stories, and from personal requests for interviews. Respondents were largely drawn from retired professionals. The form of response was via written communication, telephone, and in face-to-face interviews.

Peg suggested that Jane, as a new retiree, be the first respondent. Jane's resistance was palpable. Her internal dialogue revealed her feelings: "To be labeled a retiree is demeaning. Yes, at sixty-five, I willingly closed the doors to my professional life in Washington; I felt 'burnt out,' which made a competent commitment to my work problematic. Yes, I looked forward to 'freedom from' responsibility. I was tired, thought I needed a rest, and wanted to explore a growing interest in spiritual concepts. But I was not going to give in to the unpleasant stereotype of retirees as useless, noncontributing, 'couch potatoes.'"

Jane agreed to confront her new status and to define and describe the early internal and external changes she experienced. She wrote:

> *It is a battle between old established patterns of life and the wished for, fantasized new life . . . free, self-indulgent, reflective, with endless time to muse, read and be a different person. The impatience would be gone.*

> *. . . I feel disillusioned as much of life is the same. I am not a spiritual soul . . . I just feel questing . . . more unsettled than ever before . . . no guiding belief . . . when psychotherapy was God . . . I used to know the answers. I like this exercise. (Thank you, Peg.)*

> *I wanted to explore my inner world . . . but there are distractions . . . Isn't it a balance . . . between my need to search and enjoyment to be in this world? . . . The joy to have more time with family . . . The joys of family life to be completely present . . .*

We were enamored with the prospect of listening to the individual experiences of retirement rather than compiling broad, general statistical norms. A thematic understanding of the core issues, collected initially from a beginning sample of forty volunteers, and expanding ultimately to include over one-hundred responses, became the sustaining guide.

As Peg pondered her own views of retirement, she acknowledged that, as an artist and student, she had never lived in a nine-to-five world.

My life has been self-directed, involving a variety of activities. My periods of employment have been in flexible jobs with many varied responsibilities. When I envision my own retirement I look at it, happily, as a time to go deeper into my psyche. I will never give up my painting. Instead of full retirement at the end of a lifetime of work, I foresee both incorporating periods of retirement into my daily schedule and taking periodic sabbaticals.

Four months into gathering the interviews a car crash almost killed Jane's son and Peg's brother, David, a tragic awakening to the reality of impermanence. Jane and her husband Roger moved west to help care for him. Peg and Jane continued to communicate by computer, phone, and mail. Peg visited her brother several times, affording us time for a continued analysis of the written interviews we were receiving.

One year after we had begun our research we returned to the initial participants for follow-up phone interviews about their continuing retirement experience. At this time we expanded the pool of respondents to include face-to-face interviews with people living in the Vineyard community as well as others who offered their thoughts through published writings.

The kaleidoscope of individual experiences raised many questions about the genesis and meaning of retirement. Jane became interested in the history of retirement, especially in how it had been 'sold' to the workers in the early twentieth century. She found that many had fought against forced retirement. Peg, delighting in the imagined joys of retirement, searched for information about cultures that honored their elders, discovering that some cultures considered the late stage of life as a time for release from responsibilities, when one could seek transformation through contemplation and meditation.

Our process of inquiry expanded. We searched the historical, economic, social, gerontological, and social psychological literature. We were jarred by the realization that at the beginning of 2001 the number of people over sixty-five years of age had reached thirteen percent of the total population, whereas in 1910 they represented only four percent. We attempted to digest the power of this sizeable increase in human longevity. Listening to each person's story and reading literature from the social sciences we began to believe that retirement was a euphemism. We were dealing with the emergence of a new stage of life that included, for many, not only retirement from one's primary occupation but also a life that extended twenty to thirty years beyond retirement. The increase in human longevity had added a new rung on the ladder of human aging, a stage that seemed to represent a transition period between adulthood and the stage of old-old-age, or senescence. We identified similarities between this stage of life and that of the adolescent who transitions from childhood, struggling to find a new identity in adulthood. We named this new stage *elderescence* and it became our challenge to study and describe.

We believed that we were finally looking at the 'big picture' and proceeded to learn how our elderescents were meeting the challenges and opportunities of this new stage of life. Returning to our experiential technique of inquiry we asked, "What are the central issues facing the elderescent today?" We collected responses from elderescents in their late sixties, seventies, eighties and early nineties. Whether or not the respondent had retired or remained working he or she would still face the challenges of physical aging, eventual loss of control, and of finding one's 'place' in this stage of life.

Now, after eight years in elderescence, Jane responds with reflections on her own shifting sense of self.

I note many changes, physical, emotional, and spiritual. I go back and forth between feeling fifty and convinced that I am old. I look for a personal purpose in life. I am not quiet. I ask what is my authentic self? Coming so close to losing our son, turning to prayer, believing in prayer, I found loving kindness in meditative experience. I seek a solid understanding and acceptance of change as well as the reality of impermanence. When I do live in the moment, I feel a calm. Then I return to planning and fantasizing about what to do: manage a business, continue elderescent study, do research on non-local phenomena or distant healing, or return to work as a psychotherapist? I am clearly in what has been identified by so many of our respondents as a "betwixt and between" experience of life in change. Sometimes upon awakening I feel an anxiety that seems free floating . . . I identify it as a reaction to my life in transition, with no clear task to achieve. In minutes the anxiety leaves. I believe I will be in transition as long as I reside in elderescence. It is a new journey . . . and time is my gift to observe and reflect on the changes, the changes I see in myself and in my aging family and friends. At times it is chaotic, frightening, perplexing . . . none of these words exactly capture the sensations. There is little to draw from the past to describe the experience. There is uncertainty. Yet it does not feel like the uncertainty of adolescence, though the not knowing 'our place' is like in adolescence . . . At times I notice being treated differently; like being passed over, feeling insignificant. I ask, "Is that the pull of the ego?" I reflect . . . I feel happier when I say goodbye to the striving ego . . .

I must provide a new structure for myself . . . then comes the excitement . . . the possibilities are many, the limits are real, yet not defeating. I think of my unfinished business and the very real impermanence of my life on this earth. I feel an urgency. When I step back and muse I see many paradoxes that contribute to feeling "betwixt and between." This is a glorious time and a difficult time. I feel so involved yet more detached. I want to contribute, to offer my thoughts to the next generations. I am more with myself than ever and so present in the world. I see the beauty and marvel of life and the horrors of humankind's anger. I accept how little I know and I 'roll' more with challenges. The world looks so wide and inviting and yet I know I am dying. This is a time of opportunities for us elderescents never before granted. I know there is meaning greater than my personal life and I seek to know it. I do feel more relaxed in this stage and am enjoying the times of open spaces. I am finally resonating to the luxury of my freedom, giving up the formalities of the adult stage, and owning my authentic self. Ideas about the meaning of life get reviewed and that is 'thrilling.' Yet, at those moments, I have to monitor my 'old' wish to 'push' too hard.

As I have listened to others share their experiences living in this life transition, I have been reassured in my experiences. I honor the generous and wise respondents who allowed me to see different ways they struggled with the changes in this new stage of life. Their wisdom inspired me. Will we wake up to this gift of longer life? A dear elderescent friend in her eighty-first year shared how changed and clear she has felt since reaching eighty. I have seven more years to go! And thank you, Peg, for your inspiration.

Peg's thoughts:

What has emerged from the stories of elderescents seems important to all of us as humans. How do we find peace and meaning in the face of life as ever changing? This struggle is even more important during life's times of transition. During the writing of this book we have witnessed periods of crisis with friends and family. My brother survived a near fatal car crash; my best friend survived a mid-life change of location and work. While each individual asks the questions differently and comes to their own resolution, the experience of change is central for all. When we began this project my mother and I were ourselves in a period of transition, moving to a new community, dealing with new stations in life. Our project itself has brought meaning to us in the midst of our own periods of change.

As we shared this ongoing study through continuous dialogue and questioning, and as we continued our exploration of the literature and of our participants' responses, the naming and identification of a new stage of life emerged. This experiential approach is a process of discovery through inquiry, making one's experiences and feelings concrete through thoughtful exchanges. As our respondents opened their hearts and minds to hearing, seeing, and accepting what emerged for them, the understanding of elderescent life deepened

We loved this journey that has spanned eight years. Peg realized the fruits of the honored experiential method. Jane finally accepted her aging state and her changing sense of self, values and interests. We both enjoyed working with each other and getting to know the wonderful human beings who so generously shared their life struggles.

Thank you all.

Martha's Vineyard 2005

Acknowledgments

We express our deepest thanks to so many wonderful, generous people who offered their thoughtful reflections on living in their later years, and to others who gave us encouragement and their literary expertise in making *Elderescence, The Gift of Longevity* a reality. It is due to the responsive and enthusiastic help we received from everyone who became involved in this book, that we have been finally able to publish it.

We thank all the many elderescents who gave of their time and agreed to talk with us. Without their insights we would not have understood that this is a new stage of life and been able to describe its unique aspects and come to value its importance. Deep gratitude is offered to those who gave us permission to share their interviews in our book: Janet Frost Bank, Joanne Brandt, F. R. Burdett, Stephan Bender, Ph.D. Th.D., John Canavan, Rev. Lewis F. Cole, Jr., Walter Cronkite, Allan F. Demorest, Albert Dreyer, Ph.D., Ross Feinberg, Margaret Howe Freydberg, Don Graham (for his mother, Katharine Graham), Stan Gross, Kathleen Ann Herlihy, Rev. Walter Hillis (deceased), Russell Hoxsie, M.D., Doreen Kinsman, Paul D. Lipsitt, Henry P. Guertin-Ouellete Ph.D., Eliot Macy, Nina Chandler Murray, Leon R. Oliver, Henry Paar, Elliot S. Pierce, Ph.D., Joan Porter, Harry G. Rosenbluh (editor of Phoenician), Vincent P. Russell, Ed.D, Judith G. Singer, Thomas Sloan, Andrew H. Souerwine (deceased), Jane Stockton, Daniel G. Tear, Rose Treat, Jean and Vollis Simpson, James Weeks (deceased), Robert F. Vetter, Ernie Zimbelman, Ed.D.

A thanks to CBS for the inclusion of excerpts from two 60 Minutes shows, Mike Wallace's "Femme Fatale" and Morley Safer's "Age Wave."

Thanks to Stuart Miller for his help in conceptualizing a broader aspect of our initial effort. Thanks to Louise Wheatley and Olga Litowinsky who enthusiastically edited our first editions. And to Gayle Pearson, a stellar professional editor, who shaped our final edition into a flowing, coherent and scholarly product. Thanks to Ron Hall for his photographic assistance with our book cover.

Thanks to our loving daughter, sister, Cyndy and our friends, Bob and Erma Caldwell, and Tom and Jane Allen, who keep us going with encouragement, interest, love, and belief in our effort.

Thanks to David, our son and brother, who generously read and critiqued our first edition, always encouraging us to seek publication. And to daughter in-law and partner Sandy, who patiently supported our efforts and stressed the importance of "getting it out there."

A special thanks to our beloved husband and father, Roger, who tirelessly, with patience and love, read endless drafts, offering invaluable content suggestions and technical, and grammatical assistance over the eight years of our long journey.

Profound gratitude goes to James Kidd for the Experiential Method that provided a tool to our deepening understanding of how to beautifully research behavioral phenomena.

Part One

The Roots

THE FOCUS

If you plan to live beyond the age of sixty or sixty-five you will want to read about living in *Elderescence*, the next stage of life! You will want to know the joys and struggles of living with the gift of longevity. Maybe you have noticed the increasing number of gray heads everywhere. In fact, there are presently 35 million people over the age of sixty-five in our country. This increase has taken centuries to achieve, most of which has occurred in the last few decades. In 1910 only 4 percent of the population was over sixty-five. Today 13 percent are over the age of sixty-five. There is no other record in human history of extended longevity for millions of people. What was once the gift for a few is now the destiny of many. Since 1900 we have experienced a twenty-five-year increase in life expectancy. What are the recipients of this longevity experiencing and how are they dealing with their lives?

"Count the candles on your cake and leave!" This sarcastic remark was directed at Donald Rumsfeld, secretary of defense, when he was seventy-one years old. If such disdain for those over seventy were to prevail, Sandra Day O'Connor, with her great modulating presence and wisdom on the United States Supreme Court, would be gone. Ageism, still rampant, defeats and demoralizes the elderescent. Writing about the stigma of aging, Betty Freidan and William Butler both opened our eyes to the plight of older citizens. Aging and personal growth were thought to be incompatible.

It seems inconceivable that we in this culture would consider this extended life span a wasteland, a time of disengagement and withdrawal. As we let elderescents tell their stories in this book, we ask how they are making a 'place' for themselves in this new stage of life. In the words of President Kennedy, "It is not enough for a great nation to have added new years to life; our objective must also be to have added new life to those years."

It took our country almost a century to understand this emerging evolutionary event—extended life for so many. Mandatory retirement, instituted in the early 1900s, became the vehicle that segregated a newly formed population, *the retiree*. Today retirees are a relatively meaningless category within the population, for few retirees stay retired, some never retire, and few behave as though they are retired. When the term was first coined, however, it signified retreat, withdrawal, and death. That is hardly the picture of our elderescents today!

We began our journey in writing this book by asking newly retired, sixty-five-year-olds how they experienced retirement. After many interviews and much study and reflection, it was a fortuitous moment when we both realized that we were on the edge of understanding that we were looking at a new stage of life. The label "retirement" was simply a euphemism.

We offer the term *elderescence* to portray honor, inclusiveness, and respect for this new stage of life. It is meant to encompass a wide latitude of descriptions sensitive to the heterogeneity present. It places an emphasis on wisdom and poise rather than on oldness and frailty. *Escent* connotes the inchoate force present in this life stage—beginning and imperfect. *Essence* suggests a time when a focus on the authentic self can be developed and lived out. In the service of conceptualizing this new stage of life, some guidelines may be useful. We propose that elderescence refers to the years between sixty or sixty-five and the late eighties or early nineties, nestled between adulthood and very old age, or senescence. In the 1970s a research anthropologist honored this healthy longevity as a new era in human development, but suggested that it was accompanied by attitudes befitting people in the very last days of life. Our book will change this picture.

A valid question at this point may be, "Why add a new stage of life?" As you will see as you journey through this book, elderescents tell their own stories of change, and of feeling different during this time of life. The 'pulls' of adulthood are gone, and yet the resignation prevalent in senescence is not being experienced. Simply put, elderescents describe an awareness of changing personal characteristics, focuses, issues, and desires.

The addition of elderescence to our life cycle must be acknowledged in order to prepare for the changes it will bring, most particularly a greater involvement of elders in our society. Society and the elderescent must work toward identifying the pitfalls of extensive longevity, manage its undefined and ambiguous status, and guard against fragmentation of one's sense of self during this new stage of life. In order to embrace this new longevity it must be studied and understood. To mark this time as a different phase in the life cycle, we must frame it as a new 'rung in the ladder' of life stages.

In the early 1900s G. Stanley Hall foresaw the emergence of a new longevity and charged society "with the duty of building a new story to the structure of human life." Over the past fifty years psychologists, anthropologists, and gerontologists have advanced their awareness of this emerging evolution in human longevity. Today we hear in the words of Theodore Roszak, a noted psychologist, that longevity "is inevitable; it is the logic of progress . . . The years that longevity provides us are a resource . . . a new period of humanness . . . a new Stage . . ." He asks, "What are we going to do with all that time?"

As with the identification of *adolescence* as a new stage of life in the early 1900s, *elderescence* is the result of an evolutionary process of growth, of change, in this extended life. Like adolescence it is a transition stage. It is sandwiched between adulthood and old, old age. Identifying *elderescence* as a new stage of life calls us to focus anew, to acknowledge the gift of longevity, to ask and study what changes are experienced, what the elderescent life stage can offer humankind, and how we can help elderescents confronting these profound changes.

Whether we attribute the increase in the life span to medical technology, to retirement and increased time for leisure, to less stress, or to the laws of nature proposed by Herbert Spencer, which dictate that the strong shall survive, it is truly an evolutionary event. James Hillman, a living psychoanalyst enthralled with increased longevity, sees it also as a gift, for man's nature is a "plural complexity . . . bundles, tangles . . . that's why we need a long old age to ravel out the snarls."

Elderescents may begin by having a fantasy of freedom. Yet for some, once 'freedom from' responsibilities has been achieved, 'freedom to' becomes the challenge. Here the elderescent may need guidance in confronting the search for new meaning and purpose. Aging is undeniable. Mortality has to be faced and accepted for one to continue to live a satisfying life. Relationships change as the new 'togetherness' of partners brings joy as well as difficulties. The androgyny that emerges in this stage, for example, may be confusing to both males and females. Males may become more passive and women more assertive. To understand that this is a normal development may bring great relief.

Elderescents can 'bear witness' to what the younger generations are experiencing. As elderescents step back from the 'rat race' of contemporary life, and take time to reflect and introspect, they will find that patience and wisdom gained from a review of one's life is now possible. Over time, they may come to offer a new consciousness about the meaning of life itself and human evolution. Elderescents are fascinating people who want to continue to give and invent their new story. Theodore Roszak's words challenge and admonish us, "To date psychology has not come remotely close to mapping this later life stage."

Step One: Out of Crisis the Retiree Is Born

At the turn of the twentieth century the Institution of Retirement, with mandatory dismissal at age sixty-five, was the definitive national event that identified and segregated a new segment of our society as old and obsolete—the *retiree.* This group of citizens became the benefactors of a miraculous leap in longevity—and a new concern.

Until the late 1800s in our country, retirement was essentially a cultural opportunity decided on by the individual worker, family, or small craft industry. Landowning farmers could stop working when they chose to, establishing what we might call "informal retirement contracts" with a son or son-in-law. In exchange for the farm, the elder father and mother often continued to live in their own homes, turning over the heavy chores to the younger generation while continuing to receive necessities such as food, firewood, and other amenities until death. In some individual shops as well, when craftsmen became physically unable to continue the work pace, monies were collected for their welfare. Throughout recorded history, there have been people who in their later years retreated from labor that had become too strenuous. Biblical stories tell of aging fathers turning over birthright property to their sons. In medieval times, and even in colonial America, similar contracts were made within some families. The decision to remain working, however, decidedly remained the more prevalent and popular choice.

The subtle signs of a changing economy and an increasing work force were not entertained until three elements converged to shift the understanding of work as essential to life. First, with a rise in life expectancy, as more people began living into their forties and fifties, came the enlargement of the potential work force. Second, rapid technological changes caused the replacement of many workers by machines. By 1910 home-based businesses like shoemaking and weaving had moved to urban-centered factories. Linotype machines had changed the printing business from a craft into an industry. Some historians pinpoint 1885 as the time when laissez-faire capitalism made a lasting shift in the work place. Corporations emerged, drastically altering individual ownership of companies and of bargaining power. As people began working in large plants, individual workers lost a voice in charting their own destinies. Competition developed on a large scale, with speed as the linchpin to success. In this new rapidly paced technological world, the older worker began to be portrayed as a liability. He had to be retrained in the new technology and often had neither the speed nor the physical dexterity required to operate the new equipment.

A third factor contributing to the changing climate in the work place at the turn of the century in the U.S. was the depression of 1890. With rising unemployment and an influx of immigrant workers, older workers became expendable as a primary solution to the dire economic situation. A chief concern of the new industrial complex, the government, and the local municipalities was the number of young unemployed males who, many feared, would turn to crime in the absence of work. Several significant shifts in the public's attitudes became evident: primary among them was the changing status and power of elders in this emerging society. The evolution of change had begun. While hardly noticeable over the previous century, by the early 1900s young men had become both a subject of concern and the hope for the new technology-based society. The elevation of youth to higher status in the culture was occurring.

One solution to the economic downturn focused on finding a remedy for unemployment. The theory was that in service of technological efficiency, older workers were expendable. They represented a minority of the voting male population and, thus, their political clout was minimal. Overt age discrimination was rationalized and even condoned. There were no regulations in place for hiring or firing; dismissals were carried out strictly at the discretion of management. Shorter workweeks were created as a way to deal with unemployment, but this led to greater use of machines to speed up production, which put older workers at an even greater disadvantage as they tried to compete with younger workers.

In 1909 President Taft attempted to institutionalize retirement by proposing it become mandatory at age seventy, which effectively required the older worker to 'take the fall' for the panic of rising unemployment. World War I interfered with this plan; older workers received a temporary reprieve as young men were pulled out of the workforce and conscripted for battle. It was not until 1920, when President Wilson signed the first mandatory retirement legislation creating guidelines for firing, as well as government retirement plans for civil servants, that we had an official retirement law. The institutionalization of retirement was now underway. Few at the time appreciated its long-range consequences for future generations, that it would eventually set the stage for the emergence of a new stage of life, and the unfolding of a new human adventure in elderescence.

Business, labor, federal government, education, and various other professions all participated in the removal of older workers from the workforce. Fixed maximum hiring age limits of below forty years of age began to be enforced in many plants and factories around the country. The zeitgeist was that by removing older workers employers would benefit from greater efficiency and productivity from younger workers. Businesses, industries, firms, and organizations began to adopt an age cutoff for mandatory retirement, an enormous assault on the elderly working population. Pensions were not yet adequate. Elders who were forced to retire, and whose farms had been sold when they moved to the cities, often faced poverty in the urban centers of this emerging urban-industrial economy. This was a dilemma for employers who had personal relationships with their workers and families and felt compassion for their survival.

While mandatory retirement of the older worker was acknowledged as a lazy man's device for dealing with economic slowdown and rising unemployment, to do otherwise would have required foresight and an extensive evaluation of our growing and chaotic industrial complex. The idea of forced retirement was despised by the average worker. Fiercely independent and accustomed to structuring life with a sense of choice and individual liberty, many Americans were angry and frightened by the government's intrusion into their work lives, and threatened by inadequate pension plans. Eventually, public outcry forced government and industry to view adequate pensions as a necessity. Among Eleanor Roosevelt's private papers are testimonies from thousands of private citizens irate at mandatory retirement and in particular the poverty it often created. One memorable note to Mrs. Roosevelt reads: "You should have to live the way we do for just one day!" The financial hardship now faced by many older retired citizens was another sign of an evolving change in the demographics of our society: the creation of a new class of the poor and elderly.

President Roosevelt eventually realized that the lack of adequate financial preparation for the mandatory retirement policy needed federal intervention. The first effort at a retirement pension plan took place in the railroad companies as part of the government's move to retire 50,000 workers within that industry. The legal dialogue during hearings between an attorney for the railroad and an assistant U.S. attorney reveal the inconsistencies of the day. The attorney representing the railroads asked, "Is it right to use a deadline of sixty-five years in speaking of all classes of endeavors." In response the assistant U.S. attorney replied, "It is a common place fact that physical ability, mental alertness, and cooperativeness tend to fail after a man is sixty-five." Ironically, at the time, one Supreme Court justice was sixty; Justice Brandeis was seventy-nine. The Social Security Act was passed in 1935, marking a new phase in our history as the federal government stepped in to support the general welfare of its citizens. Privately owned companies and corporations also gradually began to offer more adequate pension plans. Workers were asked to contribute to the national pension fund. A new ideal of collective responsibility was replacing individualism. Though more humane, perhaps its purpose was also to encourage broad acceptance of mandatory retirement and to stimulate consumption among the older, non-working citizen.

However, it was not until the 1950s when public clamor, along with the lobbying efforts of trade unions and political action groups, finally secured feasible pensions for the average worker. Mandatory retirement had, in effect, by way of singling out the older worker to resolve the crisis of unemployment, created and identified a new group of citizens—the *retiree.*

From the perspective of the new retiree, attitudes openly expressed and defined by public policy in the early decades of the twentieth century had to be devastating, even demoralizing. Others, who absorbed the demeaning messages implied by these policies but were not as yet affected personally by forced retirement, could not help but observe the impact on the elderly, on their altered sense of self-worth as a result of an altered place in society.

Older citizens now confronted an unfriendly work atmosphere because their right to work was now in question. They were growing obsolete, and being asked to accept a dependent, more childlike role in society. For men, who had migrated to the city from farms, where the advice of the older experienced farmers had always been sought and appreciated, the situation was demoralizing. Anger turned to impotent depression.

As older workers faced society's changing attitudes toward them, medical science offered improvements in maternity, child birthing, and infant care. TB, typhoid fever, and smallpox were being eradicated, communities were cleaning up water supplies, and sanitation systems were installed. All this led to a decline in killer epidemics. In addition, new drugs called antibiotics were used to treat and save victims of pneumonia and influenza, and new treatments for heart disease, strokes, and cancer were beginning to prolong life spans. From 1910 to 1950 life expectancy rose by twelve years. In the early 1900s the professional community of social scientists, however, accepted the U.S. retirement policy, one of forced obsolescence, and throughout the twentieth century struggled to understand and characterize this growing population.

At first social scientists affirmed the belief that mental capacities deteriorated with aging and thus retirement, as taken from the Old French verb *retirer*, meaning to "draw back, withdraw, as in going to bed, or retreating, as in battle," was consistent with the natural stage of aging.

In 1951 a conference at the Corning Glass Works, Corning, New York, signaled the 'commencement ceremony' for a new zeitgeist in the social sciences community. Sociologists, psychologists, business, and labor management convened to discuss the social implications of retirement. As reported, Santha Rama Rau, an Indian student of Eastern and Western culture, commenting on the American workers' inability to do nothing, introduced a new way of thinking about the retirement dilemma, which included condemnation of the American attachment to a strong work ethic. She believed that retired workers should try to adjust to life without work. The not-so-subtle message was, "retiree, accept your obsolescence!"

Resistance to retirement or a poor post-retirement prognosis was considered to be the result of a lack of education about what to expect in retirement. Rather than portraying retirement as a duty to one's country and to younger workers, psychologists began to promote the message that retirement was an earned right after years of hard work, and leisure was the ideal.

Over the next twenty years social scientists presented a plethora of theories assigning behavior patterns to the retiree. The most notable theories were *activity theory, disengagement theory*, and *continuity theory*. In 1949 Roth Cavan's *activity theory* proclaimed that one's personal adjustment to retirement life required continued activity. The retiree must keep busy to remain healthy. Robert J. Havighurst restated this idea in 1963. Activity theory also may have been the seed of thought Erickson expanded upon later, in a more comprehensive form, in his book, *Vital Involvement in Old Age.*

Disengagement theory, however, which had its inception in 1951 at the Corning Conference, challenged this notion of keeping busy. Elaine Cumming, a sociologist, is officially credited with the theory of the natural, progressive withdrawal of the elderly into a passive existence (1961). In 1970 psychologists Robert Atchley and Bernice Neugarten countered with a *continuity theory,* which proposed that the maintenance of role stability led to a successful adaptation to retirement. If personal development in late adulthood was seen as consistent with development earlier in life, then the sense of self was preserved through a capacity to adapt and stay connected. Thus, if a retiree can sustain a connection with her occupational identity, she will maintain a sense of well being in spite of job loss.

Economic management of the population of retirees had been a primary motive behind the idea of retirement and subsequent mandatory retirement rules. Four decades later social scientists followed with their own theories of managing the retiree's style of life. While the social science community pondered different theories, the business community, most particularly insurance companies, was busy promoting a life of leisure and recreation.

Disengagement theory and *activity theory* ultimately coalesced to promote a commercial *sell,* glamorizing the life of leisure, and portraying retirement as a new phase of life, not an ending of life! A media frenzy ensued. Advertisements abounded for a glorious life of fun in the sun and the allure of retirement communities flooded airwaves and magazines. The American morality around the work ethic seemed to give way to a morality of fun, focusing on commercial consumption. Life insurance companies managing pension funds were one of the largest benefactors of the new emphasis on leisure.

Pressure on this new group of elderescents to fit into a certain mold has been noted in journals, including *Retirement Life* and the *National Association of Retired Civil Employees Journal.* These magazines were filled with pictures and poems of retirement parties, stories of hobbies and crafts for the retiree. The American Association for Retired Persons, established in 1955, encouraged members to remain active, or they would become a burden to their children. The idea of disengagement and keeping active made a virtue out of the dilemma of finding a new place in society for the unemployed elder. Through mass advertisement retirement became synonymous with recreation, travel, and consumption. By the late 1960s this definition of retirement life as a cultural ideal did attract some, offering them new roles, as travelers, golfers, or volunteers.

Vocal opposition to this new retirement picture, however, continued. The editor of *Lifetime Living* wrote a dissenting warning in 1980, "Leisure made sense only in rhythm with work; complete retirement, by disrupting the rhythm, created leisure in an inherently unpleasant form." In reality, the working, older American public was slow to really accept leisure as an honorable pursuit. Though a wish for leisure is an oft-reported reason given for retirement today, in 1951 only three percent of retirees stated that they had chosen retirement because they wanted leisure. In 1963 seventeen percent chose retirement because they sought a more leisurely life. Today statistics are confusing as more and more people are retiring and then returning to work. The issue of how older Americans should live out their later years is still an evolving question today!

The work ethic has been largely a consistent and primary value in our culture. Throughout world history, however, the ideal of leisure and disengagement, at least for the wealthy, was alternately valued and devalued, emerging and receding as the focus of a society changed. In the centuries B.C. the Greeks and Romans idealized the concept of leisure. In his *Politics* Aristotle suggested that a well-managed state provided leisure and freedom from the necessity of labor for its citizens. In times of prosperity, anyone unprepared for leisure would be incapacitated. The Greeks believed that the strength of a nation rested on its ability to value leisure. For them, though, leisure meant contemplation, a time to think and to cultivate a calm eye with which to view the world. Old age was depicted as peaceful, a well-earned rest from being on the go.

In medieval times the European world had returned to a predominately rural status, major cities had fallen, and the population had been drastically reduced. Rome in the second century A.D. had a population of 1,200,000. By the early Middle Ages it had dropped to 30,000. Out of necessity, the work ethic emerged as a moral imperative. Idleness and contemplation were seen as the new enemy, and freedom and prosperity were only memories. Work and craftsmanship were highly valued and few had time for leisure. Slowly, with the beginning of the Renaissance in Italy during the fourteenth and fifteenth centuries, a classical education, scholarship, the arts, and contemplation returned as honored pursuits, although the work ethic remained in place.

In rural Ireland until World War II, retirement was tantamount to a sentence of death, and was strongly condemned. In the Caucasus Mountains of Russia retirement was not even conceptualized. Old people continued to work. In colonial America the work ethic was a highly honored religious value, vital to the fabric of Protestant American life. Out of this work ethic the American culture has come to measure who one is by what one does, by how one makes a living. One is judged by the products of one's labor. Adam Smith's *Wealth of Nations* (1776) was a popular treatise, reflective of an emerging competitive colonial mind. To sit and contemplate was a luxury available only to a wealthy landowner. Leisure was seen as a state of being in which activity is performed for its own sake, not for financial or social recognition. Contemplation was antithetical to productivity. The mindset of colonial Americans about labor and leisure continued into the 1900s, making it difficult for the policy of forced retirement to gain wide acceptance.

By the mid 1900s psychological surveys of American retirees' actual experiences began to appear. Rather than attempting to explain how retirement ought to be managed, psychologists began to explore the actual reported emotional impact it had on retirees' sense of well-being. They began to observe and appreciate that this was a life-changing event often accompanied by stress. Studies in the 1940s and 1950s suggested that retirement brought an early death, a rise in alcoholism, and even a rise in the suicide rate. By the 1970s and 1980s psychological and sociological surveys were divided into two categories. The first found retirement as a generally positive experience; early death and poor health were only myths. The second identified the stressful nature of retirement and it's negative consequences.

In 1982 the Teachers Insurance Annuity Association-College Retirement Equities Fund (TIAA-CREF) conducted the most extensive survey of retirees' experiences. The survey indicated that feelings of uncertainty, aimlessness, loss of status and identity were often juxtaposed with fantasies of leisure, freedom and independence. A poll done by AARP in 1989 found that some retirees experienced feelings of denial, unbearable boredom, anger, and depression. When TIAA-CREF updated its survey in 1995, it found that the activity level of the current retiree created stress. An individual often retired for one, two, or three years and then reentered the work force, while others continued to work part time. The results of the survey emphasized the value of remaining productive.

Today many of our noted elderescents hotly debate the retirement issue. Betty Freidan in *Fountain of Age* aptly expressed the retirement paradox. "The idea of retirement is deceptive . . . it does not lead to new purposes; it can dissolve in suspiciously early death . . . or be experienced as a living death."

At seventy-two the actor Lauren Bacall spoke in a similar vein. "What is the point of being here if you're not involved? I've never understood why people spend their lives working really hard so they could retire . . . So they can stop and do nothing? Just perish? I don't get it. To me you must keep working and functioning as long as you can. When I still have curiosity and energy and want to do things and relate to others and to the world, that tells me I am alive."

Joan Rivers echoed this in her book *Bouncing Back*: "I am certainly not a puritan but I confess that the American mania for total retirement bothers me because doing nothing all day is, in the words of Cole Porter, "my idea of nothing to do."

At ninety-three Bob Hope wrote, "Retire? To what? . . . Claiming to offer uninterrupted happiness, the leisure villages have been selling a deadly narcotic to older Americans: Stop any kind of work, drop out of all meaningful activity, leave your home in a real community, and come here to have fun all the time. Well, you can't have fun if fun is all you ever have. When every day is Sunday, Sunday doesn't exist."

In 1997 Laura Pappano from the Murray Research Center at Radcliff College identified a new trend in retirement, which she termed the new retirement phenomenon. "Instead of soaking up fun, sun and midday TV . . . there is a better, more satisfying way to spend one's later years . . . Take on responsibility rather than giving it up . . . If one feels overworked, stressed, one might want a time out. But to those who have retired, the golden years can feel like the go nowhere years."

Though the big sell for a well-earned retirement found enthusiasm in the early 1970s, the storybook romance has been tarnished, and the idea of endless fun, for many, has proven empty. The stress and confusion commonly reported by retirees dealing with the prospect of twenty to thirty years of unstructured time has been compounded by the uncertainty surrounding the continued viability of Social Security.

Because of these issues, the once dichotomous pattern of being fully employed or fully retired has given way to retirement in stages, transitioning to self-employment, or taking less demanding "bridge" jobs as a way of experimenting with this new stage of life.

At the opening of the twenty-first century our social scientists are identifying slightly different issues confronting our elderescent retiree. Dora Costa in *The Evolution of Retirement* suggests "that over the course of the last century . . . retirement decisions have become less sensitive to income because retirement has become a time of discovery and personal fulfillment rather than a time of withdrawal." *Breaking the Watch* by Joel Savishinsky relates in detail the lives of 13 men and 13 women from an upstate New York community who talk about living in retirement. They speak of the diversity in their styles of adjusting to the end of the working life. "Retirement is like a progressive illness—and a spiritual expansion. There is a loss of efficacy, but the moral side grows . . . It is the gift of time, but its real burden is the re-discovery of choice, the responsibility for making up your own life."

These elderescents talk about real changes, shifts in how they live, how they experience themselves, and shifts in values. Life styles differ widely. Some will find peace in a very simple life. Some will not survive long after leaving their work; some will return to employment, probably part time. Others will not choose retirement at all. The freedom from schedules and responsibilities will be liberating to some, affording new creative endeavors. Some will change partners, others will relocate, and still others will travel extensively. In short, a retiree's adjustment will no longer be seen as contingent upon *disengagement* or *activity.*

There is no single unified behavior pattern identifying the retired elderescent, nor is there only one acceptable time to retire. We have moved from a society of managed time frames to an ephemeral one. The conventional concept of retirement no longer defines this sixty-to-ninety-year-old group, thirty-five million strong, in any meaningful way. Society's response has been awkward and limited. Lacking an understanding of the gift of longevity and perhaps without even a unified concept of the whole of life itself, our society has been unable to integrate in a new and meaningful way the growing numbers of elderescents into the mainstream. Our public conceptualization of elderescents as decaying, deformed, as objects of shame—'to be sent to the dump to be recycled'— denies us a window through which to see who elderescents really are, how they view their extended lives, and what gifts they may have to offer.

Mandatory retirement has been the means by which a new segment of our society became segregated. We have ignored the greater reality of the wonderful gift of longevity. Retirement is a euphemism for elderescence.

Step Two: "You're Over the Hill Charlie": Stereotyping and Ageism

"Would not the loss of a professor bring stimulating benefits to a university?" asked Dr. William Osler in a valedictory speech (1905) given upon his retirement from John Hopkins University at the age of fifty-six. "Effective work is done between age twenty-five and forty," he went on to say. "These are the fifteen golden years of plenty; men over sixty are seen as useless and should quit. The aged are positively dangerous, they must retire. College professors should take a year off at sixty to contemplate and then peacefully depart by chloroform!"

Clearly, Osler believed that the aging process weakened one's receptivity to change, bringing an inability to adapt to new ideas. He claimed that the problem for the aged was not deficient memory or judgment but a loss of flexibility.

His speech was not well received at the time; many believed retirement would be the sentence of death. Yet, over the next several decades, these ideas would be continually advanced, then reluctantly accepted. Elders seemed an easy target, a minority with no organized voice. Covert thoughts, over time, became overt attacks.

The mandatory retirement debate raged on in the United States well into mid century, with continued public opposition. In 1939 *The New York Times* reported that because of humanitarian sympathies, employers were not forcing enough older employees to retire. While some workers in heavy industry rejoiced in being able to retire with a pension, many felt pushed aside and unrewarded for years of dedicated work.

Resentment among younger workers increased as they grew impatient with the demands of older workers to continue working. They felt that the career opportunities that had been afforded older workers should now be theirs, creating a division between the two groups. A memorandum on pensions from a congressional subcommittee in 1931 is harshly indicative of the feelings toward the old citizen. "The old age retirement problem arises from the embarrassment management encounters in removing from the payroll those who are no longer efficient, on account of old age. The removal of human waste is more costly than the removal of material waste, because it must be done humanely."

What had been needed during this confusing period of forced retirement was a comprehensive dialogue about the future effect of forced retirement on the nation as well as on older citizens. The federal government hesitated, and no such endeavor took place. Age discrimination seemed too risky a problem to tackle.

While some older workers accepted retirement easily, for the majority being 'put out to pasture' was a painful experience. During the decades of battle over age-based mandatory retirement, age discrimination was suddenly no longer a subtle attitude held by some citizens but a recognized social policy. In 1968 Robert Butler first termed the word *ageism* to describe the negative stereotyping of old citizens as frail, senile, wrinkled, frightening, childlike, helpless, and miserable. As the chairman of the District of Columbia Advisory Commission on Aging, Butler saw stereotyping as the root of prejudicial concepts that nourished age discrimination. He pronounced *ageism* a disease requiring a cure.

Surfacing throughout human history in concrete acts of discrimination, ageism has followed the swing of a pendulum, rising and falling as values, particularly religious beliefs, and economic conditions have changed. Until the twentieth century age was revered and respected in this country. Droughts, famine, and unemployment, however, have always impacted society's treatment of the most expendable segment of the community, the elderly. Until recently, non-industrialized societies have been idealized as vigilantly honoring the elder. Social gerontologists, however, have been shedding light on what actually has happened across time in various cultures in terms of treatment of the elderly. Some of their findings confirm the image; some do not.

In the Navajo community, for instance, grandmothers teach their children that a good Navajo will always take care of the older generation. By spoiling and seducing their grandchildren into emotional attachments, they hope to ensure that they will be cared for in old age. In Gonja, West Africa, and Sania in Kenya, children are taught that, as their mother has fed them and their father has cared for them, they in turn must care for their parents when they grow old. One is severely condemned for neglecting an ailing elder in the Australian Aboriginal culture, and within the Gende people of Papua, New Guinea, and the Gusi tribe of Kenya, being left without an heir is shameful, as it leaves no one to take responsibility for the elder.

When the Twaregas of Niger suffered a three-year drought and famine, they fed the older members of the tribe first. In other tribes, however, when resources became scarce and the choice had to be made between feeding elders or children, elders were killed! Among the Maradudjara hunters and gatherers of Australia, a community always on the move in search of new hunting grounds, elders who become too weak to make the move are left behind to die. A similar code exists for the Eskimos of northern Canada. The elderly quietly slip off to the tundra or are put on an iceberg to die, taking comfort in the belief that their personhood survives in the life of a newborn.

In some cultures, old people, having survived a long life, are revered as having the wisdom of the Gods. They are said to know the secrets of life that the younger generation has not yet acquired. Some societies, however, have held the belief that older persons living on the edge of death may actually be dangerous, living in a twilight world where they can be easily influenced by the spirits of the dead, and thus able to contaminate the young. And so it was among some of the early Christians, where aging was viewed as sinful.

St. Augustine, the renowned theologian of A.D. 354–430, attributed many unpleasant characteristics to the aged. "For when life draws toward its close, the old man is full of complaint, and with no joys . . . groans abound even unto the decrepitude of old age." In his *Rhetoric* of 310 B.C, Aristotle defamed the elderly, labeling them as cowardly, hesitant, selfish, suspicious, miserly, fearful, and full of avarice. In contrast, during the plague of the Middle Ages, the elderly held the highest status because they seemed immune to the dreaded disease.

In colonial America religion dictated treatment of the elderly. Early Puritans demanded from the pulpit that respect and high regard of elders be taught and practiced, and patriarchy and veneration (meaning religious awe and reverence) honored. In the back country and among the Quakers, deference for the elderly was widespread. In each of these religious persuasions the last stage of life was revered as a time of great spiritual development as well as an opportunity to offer wisdom to one's community. "If any man is favored with long life, it is God who has lengthened his days," spoke the famous writer Increase Mather in 1716.

With the influence of materialism escalating throughout the 1800s, secularism slowly replaced religion's control. As power began to be vested in the wealthy members of the community, landowners were given the seats of honor, even in Protestant churches. By the end of the Civil War, with the growth of American industry, secular society focused on industrial production and looked to the young to provide energy and vigor for emerging industries. The slow demise of the tradition of honoring elders allowed acceptance of legalizing mandatory retirement for older workers. The elderly faced a new, sad image of themselves as portrayed by their society, and, throughout the twentieth century, ageism has been allowed to infect the common course of daily life.

With the decline in our economy in the late 1970s to the mid 1980s, a three-step process reversed the accepted theory that mandatory retirement had economic benefits and that older workers only had characteristics attributed to failure. As the labor market's demands contracted, it was thought that the removal of mandatory retirement would enhance and vitalize the economy. In 1978 the Age Discrimination Act outlawed mandatory retirement before seventy years of age. By 1986 all mandatory retirement was eliminated except for college professors who received their release from mandatory limits in 1994. A few bona fide age qualification jobs—airplane pilots, police officers, and firefighters still retain mandatory age limits. While this signaled the end of mandatory retirement, it did not end age discrimination in the work place or in society.

While negative stereotyping is often unconscious, it can be unwittingly expressed in daily life. A sixty-year-old man watches his friends enjoy kayaking and says to his son, "I think I'll try that." His son replies without really thinking, "No, Dad: you are too old!" This kind of patronizing is prevalent. At the end of a community meeting five citizens, ranging in age from thirty to seventy, were planning a fundraising event for the establishment of a teen center. Four of the members began talking about a bike trip the next day. The seventy-year-old man was conspicuously not included in the planning. He wondered, "Why?" They had all been on friendly terms for the three months they had met in each other's homes. Yet today, he was excluded from the talk about bike riding. He decided to ask if he could go along. Two of the members, age thirty-six and forty- three, turned around sheepishly, looked at him and said, "Oh, sure." One member piped up quickly, "Do you have a bike?" The older man, in fact, had been doing five-mile bike rides every other day.

If we focus on the financial burden of supporting the growing population of those over sixty, a projected 70 million by 2030, we may see this increase in longevity as a monster. Forty-year-olds may look with jaundiced eyes upon the stereotype: Mr. Jones, sixty-six, who is retired, plays golf all day, and is partly sustained by a monthly Social Security check that comes from his FICA contributions. They may agree with the Americans for Generational Equity, who tout that too much money goes to the older American, or the *New Republic* article (1988), which echoed the chorus of antipathy with these words: "The older people are an unproductive section of the population . . .one that does not even promise (as children do) one day to be productive."

Robert Butler, writing in *Why Survive?*, noted that, "Aging is the neglected stepchild of the human life cycle." Stereotyping of old people, endemic to our culture today, permits young people to view old people as different from themselves. A young person who does not identify with an old person does not have to confront the fact that he, too, will one day age and die. Most of us view the process of aging, the incapacitation of the body and often the mind, as uncontrollable and frightening. We do not wish to face our own mortality.

The devaluing of the old is blatantly reflected in our economic system. As a consumption-oriented society, we require a love affair with the new and are quick to discard the old.

Returning to the college scene we have the story of Arthur Taylor, president of Muhlenberg College in Allentown, Pennsylvania, who spoke out in favor of a return to forced retirement for professors over the age of sixty. (*New York Times*, February 16, 2000) In words reminiscent of the valedictory speech given by Dr. Osler in 1905 at John Hopkins, Dr. Taylor stated, "I truly believe that at age sixty-five, whether you go fishing or become a writer or a painter or a craftsman, you should leave a position open for a younger person." In reaction, many old professors voiced anger at his efforts to push them toward the door. One professor responded, "I feel more and more like a dinosaur . . . out of step with the new faculty . . . like an encumbrance to the plans of the new administrator. He would just like to see those nearing retirement to get out as soon as possible."

One year earlier, in January 1999, the U.S. Supreme Court supported a ruling that effectively continued to deny redress for state employees who face age discrimination. The AARP reported that "In a five-four decision that generated bitter controversy and could have far reaching implications for many types of age bias cases, the majority held that state employees may not sue state governments for age discrimination in federal courts." The court took the position that, "Old age does not define a discrete and insular minority because all persons, if they live out their normal life spans, will experience it." AARP and

seven other groups opposed this ruling, stating that, "Old age is a status as immutable as race or sex. Age is a status you cannot choose.
Once you are there, there is no going back." Indeed! When states are
accused of age discrimination, when they do not protect parity for aging, the employee has no recourse to the federal government.

In February 2003, age bias complaints were reported to be up 40
percent since 1999, from 14,000 to 20,000. David Grinberg reports in
the AARP Bulletin that it "is linked to a confluence of factors . . . more
older people staying on the job longer, the economic downturn that has
led to worker layoffs . . . and simply blatant discrimination based on
age." Today, ageism is identified as one of the last areas of discrimination to be dealt with responsibly. Aging is in our DNA, and ageism
is in our cultural DNA. Some young people may envy the thought of
retirement, but they do not usually envy getting old.

Older people are often their own worst enemies. They will tell you
getting old is "hideous, don't kid yourself!" We fear aging, perhaps because of the isolation, demoralization, and frailty it surely will bring,
along with the effects of these changes on one's sense of self. To imagine living for twenty to thirty more years burdened by these limitations
is depressing. Because so many of our cultural woes are projected onto
older citizens, a desensitizing process may be necessary, allowing citizens old, young, and everywhere in between to really look at active,
energetic, wise, and, yes, wrinkled elders who are making phenomenal
contributions to the world.

The American Association of Retired Persons calls for older citizens
themselves to speak out in the fight against ageism. Around 60 B.C. Cicero proclaimed, "Old age is respectable just as long as it asserts itself,
maintains its proper rights, and is not enslaved to anyone." A psychologist speaks out today with optimism: "Elders are a vital subplot in the
larger human story . . . they are necessary for the well-being of all age
groups, particularly the young."

At seventy-five, Adeline McConnell, a contributor to *Woman's Day,*
declared her love of being old in a simple but succinct way. "Not senior, not golden-aged, not chronologically gifted, as my grocery store
clerk would like to call me . . . Just plain old will do for me. Like black,
it's beautiful." On October 1, 2002 Robert Butler, still one of the
strongest proponents of the war against ageism, gave a powerful
speech at a conference on aging about the need to fight the denial of

ageism and the necessity to find the purpose and meaning in elderescence. In *Fountain of Age* (1993) Betty Freidan speaks with optimism about psychologists and psychiatrists who are now challenging the destructive myths of aging in their research endeavors and in new therapeutic approaches.

Is society at large ready for this shift in consciousness about our aging population? A shift *is* needed if this new stage of life is to become valued and thus viable.

Step Three: Elderescence—Accepting a New Stage of Life

We talk about the increased longevity of human life over the last century as a source of concern, delight, study, and even wonderment. We are living many years beyond a 'working life.' Yet, we cannot contend with this evolutionary leap until we identify the issues and facts that are a part of the trend toward greater longevity, including the pitfalls, i.e., the widely held belief that older people should retreat and die. In the past this belief has defeated many an elderescent. We hope it is not too optimistic to suggest that over the past two decades this message has begun to change, encouraging our elderescents to stay active and believe in themselves. Robert Butler seems to end this debate in 2002 with, "retirement has been a 20th century aberration."

News articles abound with advice on what to do with the additional years. The headline of the December 2002 AARP newsletter reads, "Trend Toward Longer Life Leads many Americans to Re-invent their Retirement." Elderescent retirees *are* "rethinking and revitalizing" their lives, and are doing amazing things in their later years. When asked about fearing global aging, Koifi Annan, secretary-general of the U.N., replied, "I wouldn't use the word 'fear.' Global aging is a potential pool of untapped resources that societies must learn to pursue in a productive way. In the developed world, more and more people are moving into the aging category and there is a shortage of workers. They can use the talents of these mature people."

He spoke about the plight of older citizens in less developed countries and expressed his commitment to monitor governments in their efforts to introduce "right policies in relation to aging." When asked whether he thought about aging himself, he responded, "When I was 31 or 32 . . . started asking myself . . . who am I? And why am I here?

Where am I going? . . . I think I'm still searching. (chuckles) It's a life-time search."

"Longer life is driving the trend," suggests Dr. Quinn, professor at Boston University. Perhaps he has "put the cart before the horse." More importantly, we must ask what meaning living longer might hold for humankind.

References to the emergence of a new stage of life began in the early 1900s when G. Stanley Hall in *Senescence* projected an 'Indian Summer' of life, noting that "it is ours to complete the drama . . . to add a new story to the life of man, for as yet we do not know what full maturity really is . . . to offer the wisdom that long life gives . . . heir of all the ages, man has not yet come into his full heritage." In the mid-1900s Carl Jung and Erik Erickson referred to a vision of a new stage of life.

We have chosen to honor Dr. Margaret Clark, a senior research anthropologist, who in 1972 was the first to proclaim that culture in the United States had indeed, produced a new life era. She believed this phenomenon was an outgrowth of a "healthy longevity, extended by a quarter of a century after the rite of passage of retirement from adult occupations and responsibilities, (but was) accompanied by social attitudes appropriate only toward those in the very last days of life."

Stages of life have fascinated mankind since perhaps the beginning of the written word. Nearly every culture and spiritual tradition has tried to identify human development by delineating life stages. In the Hindu tradition, the first stage of life is *brahmucharya* or celibacy, the period of learning and ego development associated with childhood and young adulthood. The second stage is *garhastha*, or, "living as a householder." This is a time of being in the world, developing an ego-identity, and enjoying the "bittersweet fruits" of the world. The third stage is *banaprasha*, a period of withdrawal, of looking inward and cultivating an awakening of Buddhi. In this stage the Hindu seeks life in the forest, leaving his family behind to enter a period of contemplation and spiritual retreat. The fourth stage, *sanyas* or renunciation, is a time of transcendence of all dualities, all drives, in order to experience final liberation. The Buddhist tradition offers a similar understanding of the life course, the final stage again reflecting a time of spiritual retreat and meditation.

In the Western world, many psychologists, writers, and sociologists have attempted to define our life stages. Eugene Meyer (father of

Katharine Graham), entrepreneur and publisher of the Washington Post before his death, offered a succinct outline of the stages of life as he saw them, and the tasks each stage would present, reflecting the simplicity of Eastern thinking. Meyer saw each stage as identified by a specific role which related to age. The model for his vision was William Edward Hartpole Lecky's *Map of Life.* Lecky believed that "A man's life should be planned as a single whole in which each stage would be a prologue to the stage that followed."

The first stage of life, up to age twenty, was designated the *school years*, with education as the task. The years from twenty to forty were to be a period of *growth and experimentation;* one's task was to plan to develop a business, become competent at something, or make millions and marry. The years from forty to sixty were to be dedicated to *implementing,* putting into practice what one had learned, and devoting one's time to public service. Finally, people between the ages of sixty and eighty would be expected to *grow old gracefully*, mentoring young people while gradually relinquishing decision making to the younger generation.

Gail Sheehy, author of *Passages: Predictable Crises of Adult Life* and *New Passages: Mapping Your Life Across Time,* proposed adulthood be divided into two broad stages, twenty to forty-five and forty-five to sixty-five, the latter being a stage she identified as the Age of Mastery or middlescence, which is dominated by ego striving for success. The Age of Integrity, sixty to eighty-five, came last.

In *Adaptation to Life* by the psychologist George Vaillant, the author, in trying to understand the stages of life, followed the lives of 268 undergraduates into their fifties (1937–1947), interviewing his subjects and analyzing the information. Vaillant sadly concluded, "This was not to be! The life cycle is more than an invariant sequence of stages with single predictable outcomes. Rather, the study of lifetimes is comparable to the study of celestial navigation. Neither a sextant nor a celestial map can predict where we should go; but both are invaluable in letting us identify where we are." He assessed that the pinnacle of life was in the mid-forties.

Daniel Levinson wrote two books, *A Season of a Man's Life* and *A Season of a Woman's Life*, based on thirty years of research. (His wife completed the second book after his death in 1996.) Levinson refers to *eras* rather than *stages* of life, acknowledging the fuzzy overlap not accounted for in most stage theories. He sees the first era as including birth, childhood and adolescence, a time when *me* is distinguished from *not me*. The second era, early adulthood, from seventeen to forty-five, is a time of abundant energy, striving and stress. The third era, middle adulthood, forty to sixty-five, is a period of greater maturity. As one enters senior 'citizenhood,' biological capacities begin to dwindle and one experiences a growing sense of emptiness. The fourth life era, late adulthood, begins at sixty and includes a period of transition from sixty to sixty-five. The last life era is late, late adulthood, and begins at age eighty.

Levinson's work identified two central themes that signify the growth and decline or ups and downs of the journey through life. These are 'adolescing' and 'senescing' and can occur periodically across the life course. That is, though childhood is mostly a time of 'adolescing', there can be moments of 'senescing.' Some vital 'adolescing' may be done toward the end of the life cycle as one seeks to obtain fuller meaning in one's life. Levinson indicates that in adulthood one can experience an interplay of 'adolescing' and 'senescing,' growth and decline.

Levinson's work is unique in bringing flexibility to the structure of the life cycle, with an understanding that eras and issues overlap. Still, Levinson offers few details about the late adulthood era, from sixty-five to ninety. This is undoubtedly because he wrote that at sixty only 'old age' remains. At best, according to his views, the sixty-year-old can grandparent, and be a source of indulgence, but his work life, and other activities that made life worthwhile, are over. He must come to terms with the self . . . be ready to give it up and prepare for death. For Levinson, there is little overlap in the late adulthood era: one is either youthful or old.

Erik Erickson, the celebrated scholar of the psycho-social stages of life and renowned authority on human development *(Childhood and Society, The Life Cycle Completed,* and *Vital Involvement in Old Age)*, delineated eight stages of psycho-social development: infancy, early childhood, play age, school age, adolescence, young adulthood, adulthood, and old age. He also offered the most comprehensive study of the meaning of life stages, the themes and issues that were central to each stage.

In Erickson's two final stages of life, adulthood and old age, two opposing dispositions were identified; the theme generativity, meaning the need to take care of what has been procreated, is juxtaposed with the theme of stagnation. If reaching out to care for others is not achieved, then stagnation occurs. In Erickson's old age stage, the last struggle of life is one between integrity and despair. Wisdom and integrity are seen as the strengths of old age, when one must develop an integrated sense of self that allows "one to accept one's past, present and future . . . the acceptance of one's one and only life cycle as something that had to be." This must be balanced with the tendency to fall into despair. Erickson's old age stage spanned the early seventies to the late nineties.

In 1980 Erickson became very aware of the increase in human longevity and wrote, "as time goes on and the number of older citizens increases . . . the designation of some age as the norm for this crossing over into old age may be necessary . . . By relegating this growing segment of the population to the onlooker bleachers of our society, we have classified them as unproductive . . . Surely, the search for some way of including what they can still contribute to the social order in a way befitting their capacities is appropriate and in order."

Erickson speculated about the possibility of a new stage of life emerging some day. We believe if he were alive today he would sanction the elderescent stage of life. In reaching his eighties, Erickson began to speculate that "as time goes on and the number of older citizens increases . . . there would be a need for a ninth life stage." Erickson obviously was appreciating his continued productiveness and gifts to social science well into his eighties. After hip surgery, at the age of ninety-one, he reportedly "became withdrawn and serenely retired." He was not considered to be depressed or bewildered, but quietly observant and appreciative,—"gracious about old age." In 1994, he died at the age of ninety-two.

Both Erik Erickson and his wife Joan were dedicated to understanding the progression of human development across a lifetime, and offered us the first comprehensive, researched study of the meaning of life stages. Up to the very end of both their lives they continued to revise their understanding of the stages of human development. Erik Erickson was on the verge of acknowledging the need for a new look at the post-adult life when he died. Joan Erickson revised his *The Life Cycle Completed* in 1997, adding the ninth stage of life that Erik had first mentioned in the 1986 book *Vital Involvement in Old Age*. In this ninth stage, the years eighty to ninety, Joan Erickson focused on the process of gero-transcendence, a shift in perspective from material concerns to a cosmic or transcendant focus.

The above noted scholars of the stages of life, Vaillant, Levinson, Sheehy, the Ericksons, and Myers began their studies in the 1940s and 50s, when a belief in a major extension of the life span could only have been a fantasy. In spite of that they did offer some preliminary characteristics of the elderescent stage that seem accurate today. Meyers mentions "growing old gracefully," and suggests mentoring, but advises stepping back from the reins of decision making. Sheehy calls the sixty to eighty-five year life stage "the Age of Integrity," as did Erickson. Vaillant despaired that there would not be much of life left after the forties. Levinson, apparently valuing adolescing (meaning growth) as a process, suggested that adolescing may also be done toward the end of life as one seeks to obtain fuller meaning in life.

The process of identifying elderescence now in some ways mimics the efforts to identify and acknowledge adolescence as a new life stage in the early 1900s. G. Stanley Hall, who was the first social scientist to define adolescence in his two-volume book, *Adolescence* (1904), spoke of it as a "sandwich" stage, emerging as an extension of childhood and lasting through the teen years. It was identified as an outgrowth of the economic atmosphere of the time, one that supported the delay in the start of a work life for a teenager, providing an elongated period of educational opportunity. Hall called this time in one's life *storm and stress,* a period of transition and ambiguity. It took decades before society would understand and appreciate both the inherent stress and the opportunities for growth in the adolescent stage, and before it would attempt to provide special emotional support for those in its throes. Prior to this, adolescents were on their own, often relying on experimentation as a way to discover the meaning of this period in life. As society's expectations merged with the intrinsic needs of the teenager, this stage became a valued one, and the chaos and confusion better tolerated.

Erickson identified the crisis of self-definition that is applicable to both adolescence and elderescence. The elder "faces the task of bringing identity and a sense of identity diffusion into balance by seeking to make sense of the self that has lived through many decades, that lives in the present, and that will continue to live in the indeterminate future . . . Old age's reconciling of the tension between identity and identity confusion re-involves the individual in the psychosocial process that dominated adolescence."

Critical to the emerging sense of self in adolescence are the development of a personal ideology, the questioning and rejecting of beliefs interjected from the family, and the fashioning of one's own belief system. One concrete way to resolve the crisis of self-definition is to commit oneself to a role, often an occupational choice for an adolescent. In contrast, for elderescents self-definition reoccurs as one's work life diminishes. Since the conception of institutionalized retirement, society has tried to define elderescents by supplying them with new roles, "jobs" if you will, by advising them to "rest, play, volunteer, be happy, and silent." Today elderescents themselves are involved in this struggle of self-definition, finding ways to remain unique and valuable, and to make a difference.

We can learn much from examining the dynamics of these two life stages. As in adolescence, the elderescent stage is a transition, a time of experimentation, an opportunity to understand the changes inherent to this period, a time in which to educate oneself, undertake new activities, discover new roles—all a part of finding one's new identity.

While the community has offered guidance and support for both adolescence (a time of *storm and stress*) and elderescence (a time of being *betwixt and between)* there is a subtle difference in the attention and concern the two groups are afforded. Adolescents are seen as the "hope of the future," with a long life span ahead. In contrast, elderescents are considered to have only a few years left in which to go, as in Dylan Thomas' words, "gently into the night."

There is a startling parallel between the economic influences at work during the time these two groups, adolescents and elderescents, emerged. Both are outgrowths of the Industrial Revolution, which eventually created both an economy and a technology that could support retirement and prolong childhood and old age. Work issues are central to both groups. Because our culture places a high value on professional identity, one of the tasks of adolescence in our society is understanding and accepting that one's identity is connected to the work one does. The retired elderescent, on the other hand, is faced with giving up a job identity and thus seeking a new sense of self.

While adolescence is a movement away from the state of childhood into adulthood, elderescence is a transition from adulthood to the state of senescence. Both transitions require a redefinition of one's self in relation to one's peers, family, and societal demands. The adolescent's struggle for an identity separate from family is often acknowledged as profound and tumultuous. As his identity becomes defined, values are assumed and solidified by the choices made. The adolescent's answer to the question "Who am I?" will define his choice of work, relationships, and purpose in life.

These same questions are confronted again by elderescents in retirement. "Who am I now? What do I want to do? What will be meaningful now?" This struggle can be as tumultuous for the retired elderescent as it is for the adolescent. The achievement of personal integrity is essential to both groups. The adolescent must learn to use projection in order to externalize negative feelings that may result from this struggle, thereby protecting his still tender sense of identity on his journey to self-acceptance. Elderescents, on the other hand, are able to internalize the projections that result from the self-evaluation required during this stage of the journey.

As elderescents leave the work world behind, they experience not only the loss of their positions in life but also of friends, a familiar environment, and structure. Adolescents experience losses too as they leave the stage of childhood behind. Playtime activities are given up in order to develop new interests and friends. Also, family members may begin to treat both elderescents and adolescents differently. While the community may view adolescents as young adults who need to take more responsibility, it may perceive elderescents as deserving of less personal responsibility. Confusion and uncertainty may result for both adolescents and elderescents as they struggle to understand societal expectations and to determine their own wants and needs.

Both stages become unique times of choice and decision making. Each is a transition requiring individuals to evaluate changes and to make decisions about how to meet these changes. But, though the content of the struggle is similar, these changes will take adolescents and elderescents in seemingly opposite directions. For adolescents, the relationships outside the family become more important as they leave behind the shelter of home, while for elderescents, family relationships become more important as the work environment is left behind. And, while elderescents are cutting back on moneymaking endeavors, adolescents are beginning to seek part-time jobs and beginning to relish earning their own money.

Adolescents become more conscious of dress and fashion. Elderescents gradually care less about being in style, with style of dress more determined by convenience. While organized religion is often not important for adolescents, for some elderescents church-based activities may gain importance, or they may search for new spiritual direction and meaning.

Significant, unavoidable physical changes are central features of each of these life stages, often causing pain and stress, and bringing further erosion of one's sense of identity. The pubescent adolescent experiences growth spurts, boys' voices change, and both boys and girls go through hormonal changes, with new interest in sex. Teenage boys anxiously look in the mirror hoping to find whiskers. Both boys and girls are distressed by the appearance of pimples. Similarly, the elderescent scans the mirror for new wrinkles and brown spots, and experiences a decrease in physical stature and disturbing changes in sexual function.

Both adolescents and elderescents may experience consummate anxiety about who they are becoming. The adolescent hopes that life will get better, that the pimples will disappear. The elderescent must adjust to the inevitable changes,—more gray hair and wrinkles.

There is a message to be found in the *Adventures of Alice in Wonderland* by Lewis Carroll. After disappearing down the rabbit hole, Alice first shrinks to about ten inches, then, moments later, expands to normal size. "Goodbye feet!" she said. "Oh my poor little feet, I wonder who will put your shoes and stockings on for you now, dears? I'm sure I shan't be able! I shall be a great deal too far off to trouble myself about you." Later, when she met up with the caterpillar, he asked, "Who are you?" she stammered, "I—I hardly know sir, just at present . . . at least I know who I was when I got up this morning, but I think I must have been changed several times since then." When the caterpillar asked, "What do you mean by that? Explain yourself." She said, "I can't explain myself; I'm afraid sir, because I'm not myself, you see."

Society offers ambiguous messages to both adolescents and elderescents. At times the teenager is treated as a child, i.e., he must abide by parental limits, and at other times he is given the responsibilities of an adult. This can cause conflict and confusion for adolescent and parent alike. "Take the car but be home by midnight or else!" says the parent.

Similarly, the status of the elderescent can change from moment to moment. Sometimes elders are given full responsibility and authority and are expected to manage their affairs independently. At other times an aging person needs care and protection. Offering these things when they're not warranted, however, can leave an elder feeling demeaned and irritated. Society's expectations of both elders and teens can be inconsistent. The closer the teen is to childhood, the more ambiguous the message. The same is true of elderescents. The closer the elderescent gets to senescence the likelier it is society will attempt to intervene, whether or not it's warranted.

Transformations in human development have often been recognized only in retrospect. Perhaps only when the achievements resulting from evolution have been documented do we acknowledge the changes as authentic. To understand what has emerged requires "the bigger picture," a view of history and of social/ political events as well as a study of the present. To fully grasp the meaning of change requires some distance from the events themselves and reflection over time.

The field of quantum physics, slowly coming into existence throughout the past century, has only recently been acknowledged and accepted by the scientific community as well as the general public. These new concepts have revolutionized our understanding of atomic and subatomic structure, of our universe, the cosmos, and human consciousness itself. Albert Einstein, Niels Bohr, Werner Heisenberg, and others have helped us to understand that concepts of time and space are our own inventions, products of our own senses. A "timeless, flowing field of constant transformation" is replacing the space/ time paradigm. Such a worldview permits us to appreciate everything in the cosmos, including humankind, as a constantly changing interconnected oneness, as "a flowing organism empowered by millions of years of intelligence . . . dedicated to overseeing the constant change that takes place inside you." (Deepak Chopra).

This perspective has allowed us to accept a shift in our understanding of human consciousness and of an evolving perspective that accepts change and impermanence as central to our continuing life story. Sometimes it takes us a century or longer to recognize that an evolutionary change has occurred or that a change is in process. Recently we have learned from the advances in telescope technology that our cosmos is ever expanding, even accelerating.

When we look at human development from a simple physical perspective, we see that the structure of the human body has changed over time from a body frame of three feet to an average size today of five feet six inches. Human intelligence has expanded as well, developing in ways never dreamed of even three or four centuries ago. One has only to look back to an earlier period in one's own life to recognize one's own development, to observe the changes experienced and the maturity acquired over the intervening years. For some of us this review may be astounding. Life does not stand still. Evolution, with its advancements in science, health, consciousness, and societal structures, is profound and ceaseless, and its effect on the human life span is no exception.

We predict the emergence during the 21st century of great possibilities for elderescents in how to creatively live their lives and for an expansion of roles—ones that have not yet been dreamed of. William Butler suggests our culture is not adequately prepared for this new stage of life. Accepting this new longevity will demand a huge shift in consciousness as elderescents travel a terrain not previously mapped. It is also essential that elderescents themselves acknowledge this new stage of life so that they can reflect on the changing face of their world, offer to others a new consciousness about life, provide wisdom to the younger generations, and, perhaps, face the inevitability of death with greater assurance.

Part Two

The Early Years of Elderescence:
Betwixt and Between

A DIFFERENT HORIZON: DEALING WITH CHANGE

Transitioning into a new stage of life may be experienced gradually but the awareness of change may be abrupt. Signs of these changes may be characterized by new interests, values, or pursuits, as well as by an awareness of physical changes or a shift in consciousness. The shift in sense of self, though not often noted initially, will play a central role in how one manages this transition process. Although each person's story is unique, there is one universal experience for the elderescent—*change*.

Ram Dass succinctly notes a paradox embedded in the concept of change: "Changes can engender exhilaration and be profoundly frightening. When it happens to who we think we are the fascination turns to fear."

While there is a wide spectrum of specific documented changes that may take place during major transitions in life, the fact that change has occurred is undeniable. This can be terrifying, causing contraction, feelings of not wanting to let go of what has been, of what is familiar, including our sense of self. And yet, as Richard Moss said, "If we try to hold on to a concrete or absolute sense of ourselves as the winds begin to erode the outer fringes of our being, the change brings fear. It is the illusion of ME that brings the pain." Whether these experiences become traumatic or challenging and exciting varies with each individual.

The first profound change for many elderescents is retirement. As we noted in Part One, retirement life is a very different experience now than it was in the early 1900s. Elderescents who retire now, barring health issues, do so usually because they choose to. The trend now seems to be drifting even further away from retirement, or retiring temporarily and then returning to work.

The motivation for retirement is sometimes expressed as a need for change from one's life work/ profession. Elderescents have different desires and goals than they did as younger adults, motivating them to work less, not at all, or change professional identities.

Many elderescents identify the freedom that this time of life affords them, a freedom once only dreamed of but now a distinct possibility. In *The Gift of Time* (1997), Carol Heilbrun, a professor of English at Columbia University, expressed joy at the freedom suddenly available to her upon her retirement at the age of seventy. "I entered a life unimagined previously, of happiness impossible to youth or to the years of being constantly needed both at home and at work. I entered into a period of freedom . . . to live without a constant unnoticed stream of anger and resentment."

Many elderescents identify freedom as the most important component of their new lives. A retired consultant remembers, "I was ready to smell the roses as it were; I enjoy travel, music, seeing people in settings other than my office, dating, writing ad infinitum." A former businessman expresses his feelings as "an almost unmitigated feeling of release, from demands of scheduling activities, from profession and job commitments, from responsibilities for other workers." Doing what you want, when you want, is the essence of these initial feelings of joy.

Life of an RV Retiree

Unencumbered by responsibility, one million retired Americans have found their freedom "on the road," as recreational vehicles, or "RVs" have become one of the primary joys of retirement life.

The following story is a prime example of the elderescent focus on freedom.

Ricky is an elderescent retiree from the federal government. After establishing financial security, he relates that his next task was to decide how to spend his new-found time. He had also become aware of the disappointment experienced by friends who had decided to spend their elderescent years skiing, golfing, fishing, and gardening. They found no lasting contentment.

Ricky believes that there are only two keys to keeping one "spiritually alive, especially after a stimulating career. Number one—keep on working. If you love what you do continue to work or volunteer, go back to school, start a business, or write a book. Number two—do full time travel, more than a million people live on the road today." Ricky and his wife chose the second option. "Traveling around the country . . . (we) have become students of history, geography, language, arts and crafts, and human nature. We have stood on the ramparts at Fort Sumter and watched, in our minds, as the noisy, smoky battle unfolded before us. In Lincoln, Nebraska, we stood on the stairs facing the bullet hole in the wall where Billy the Kid shot Deputy Bell."

"During our travels we meet hundreds of wonderful . . . extraordinary people . . . The best part is that everyone is equal out here . . . doctors, farmers, automotive executives, city workers, authors . . .We met an eighty year old couple who has been on the road twenty five years and they still have no desire to settle down. Like work, full time travel can be an all-consuming passion."

The RV communities fiercely guard their freedom to just "pick up and go." While some RV'ers eventually select to settle down into one RV site for an extended time, the RV life offers great variety to others who are more restless—who put a priority on movement, freedom, and the fellowship of "the open road."

Rick searched for a retirement solution that would keep him spiritually alive and feeling free. The RV life is obviously a life that fits some temperaments and not others. For some, it perhaps is an answer to feelings of restlessness, of "being stuck," or of going backward by always having the sensation of moving forward. RV'ers have few responsibilities and can presumably do whatever they want when they want to. This group of elderescents meets the challenge of change by living in the moment.

In no other life stage is freedom a possibility for so many, especially for those who have achieved on-the-job success and attained financial security. Some elderescents experience freedom from the external demands of a job, however, as only a small component of their sustained sense of freedom.

J. W. Fowler writes in *Becoming Adult, Becoming Christian: Adult Development*, "Freed from the burden of justifying their lives with their works and liberated from the intensifying cycle of self-absorption that obsessive self actualization requires, they have the internal freedom to take new risks and to initiate new roles and projects."

After the fantasy of infinite joy during retirement fades a bit, many retirees, finding endless freedom a burden, find themselves asking the question, "What do I want to do now?" In the words of one woman, struggling with how to find meaning without work: "For the last three months I enjoyed the solitude, doing whatever I felt like whenever I felt like it . . . Now I feel restless . . . I find myself with too much time on my hands and not enough to do with it . . . I'm always looking for things to do to take up all the free time I have."

It may be that freedom for some can only be appreciated and enjoyed within the framework of some amount of structure. Instead, with the sudden release from demanding work schedules, most elderescents are plunged into endless unstructured time. At first, the urge for freedom can propel most elders into wanting to "do it all," a serious pitfall in early retirement. If time isn't taken to experiment, assess activities for meaning, and recognize and establish priorities, many elderescents may end up in activities that fill time but lead to meaningless and unsatisfying experiences. Many voice this refrain: "I am surprised to find how busy I have been this year, doing next to nothing. I do not know how I ever found time to work for a living. I am doing full time what I used to do for recreation when I was working."

Most people live their lives by the 'clock.' Time, a pure abstraction, is internalized so powerfully by so many that it assumes a meaning of its own. Thus, while there may be a deep sense of freedom from structure in retirement, a new retiree's orientation in time and space can be seriously disrupted, particularly because we use the concept of time to separate past, present, and future.

These phenomenological shifts can cause uncertainty. Without discipline the elderescent may expend his time in blocks that are short and discrete, ten minutes on the phone, an hour of shopping, coffee with a friend, a two-hour meeting . . . In the absence of a daily schedule, interruptions are permitted or encouraged, further splintering a day and causing greater stress. The elderescent wonders at the end of the day: "What happened to the time? What have I accomplished?" Managing unstructured time can be more stressful than putting in long hours on the job, where one knows what to expect and has a chance to settle in to the experience.

Endless unstructured time, though, can also be a positive experience, as expressed by this retiree: "I love the luxury of having time . . . without an event, time simply ceases to exist." A sense of 'freedom to,' accompanied by an awareness of one's internally directed purpose, can be a powerful experience. Time becomes a gift not a burden, providing space in which to reflect and know one's self again free from external distractions and demands, free from pretense, roles and expectations, and from demands on how one should behave. Time, experienced like this, can give the elderescent a solid identity at the end of the "betwixt and between" struggle.

It should be emphasized that elderescents today are achieving more control over their own destiny. One elderescent proclaims, "God is pleased with me for having discovered human freedom and does not care that I left my first vocation . . . I can feel free to do what I wish!" Another explains, "It is an evolution of not only physical longevity, but emotional, psychological, and energy-wise transformation. It is a total organism evolution. This stage necessitates a direct dealing with Death."

There is no doubt that many elderescents do recognize and can describe internal shifts in their attitudes and focus as they move from the adult stage of life into elderescence. In contrast to the 1950s, when social scientists defined the needs of elderescents, social scientists are now listening and learning themselves, and elderescents are willingly sharing their insights.

As noted earlier, while the initial period of retirement can be described as joyous, hopes and aspirations often fade as time advances. Without a work identity the elderescent's place in his world, as well as in his relationships, can be turned upside down. Elderescents may not only experience the loss of their old identities but also the underlying structure of their lives as well.

One elderescent captures this dynamic: "Because of not having the structure and identification that comes with work, there are times of anxiety and self-doubt. I have seen my days not as having possibilities but as being a huge emptiness and my part as being meaningless."

According to Ann Harsten of the Needham Massachusetts Council on Aging, many do not understand this process. "There is a major transition that occurs when you stop working and retire. The realization stops people in their tracks." This is why these changes have to be talked about, acknowledged, and identified in the understanding of a new stage of life.

For many, the first few years of retirement are often times of floundering, uncertainty, and unexpected anxiety. An elderescent psychotherapist, retired for four months, describes being struck with extreme anxiety, almost to the level of panic. "I have nothing to hang on to . . ." This realization uncovered for him what he had been denying. He no longer had an identifiable purpose in his community, one to which he could feel anchored.

In his gentle *Retirement Journal*, John Mosedale reports that, "When I walked out of the CBS Studio 47 for the last time as a worker there, I headed into the future that no longer defined itself in a news room . . . I'm on my own, to make a new life, not a living . . . I tell myself I have a wife, children . . . etc., and yet . . . there remains that great space which I filled by writing news." He offered the wise words of Pascal, "the silence of these infinite spaces terrifies me." "I think," says Mosedale, "that is what the idea of retirement means . . . a sudden silence after the roar of work."

Others talk about a new understanding of life based on the ability to accept change. "The challenge is to put new meaning in place of that which work provided. There is a sense of loss of momentum and of focus." One businesswoman offers, "Being retired is, as I suspect with most people, a mixed bag. There was no sudden jolt of being employed one day and then retired the next. That made the transition much easier, with a gradual winding down. Change is difficult and retirement is no different from any other life-altering event. You learn to adapt, put aside that which is gone and move on to new adventures."

A teacher who moved to her "island paradise" after retiring expresses unequivocal pleasure in the changes. "This past year is the happiest in my life." A retired elderescent chemist identifies this time as a transition phase, one in which she will look for a new focus. It is, "Another chapter . . . with possibilities for moving to a new community and pursuing work completely different from that done before retirement . . . Another short story in the series of my life."

Optimism, excitement about what the future can bring, a honeymoon period, fear of the unknown, disillusionment at the emptiness that follows, anxiety about the inevitable uncertainties; all these are feelings that have been reported by elderescents in the initial few years after retirement. Experimentation comes in the service of seeking a new life. "All our lives we are engaged in the process of accommodating," pronounces Butler. Retirement is not a state but a process, marking a transition toward a new life stage—elderescence.

In his book, *Transitions*, the psychologist William Bridges speaks of the experience of transition as consisting of several phases. We have applied this model to the elderescent experience after retirement. Bridges identifies the first phase as the *ending* phase. For the retiree this is the leaving behind of one's work. Bridges sees this as often followed by periods of disconnection, uncertainty and despair, which he labels the *neutral zone*, an in-between time. The retiree is deprived of old identities and connections. Uncertainty may be expressed in feelings of doubt about whether or not they should have retired. Bridges advises that those in transition must truly mourn the old before a new beginning can be made.

Some retired elderescents seem to traverse this phase rapidly, involving themselves immediately in new activities. They may describe constant busyness and travel, actually circumventing the natural mourning process. Others who talk of a loss of momentum, of being a has-been, may be deep in Bridge's neutral zone, lingering on the edge of unacknowledged mourning.

Accompanying the transition from work life to retirement status is often the rude phenomenon of being seen as old! The aging process further erodes one's sense of identity. In *Fountain of Age,* Betty Freidan so clearly describes this erosion. "The assumption that we will all one day stop working, either by choice or because we are compelled to do so, has long been a fact of life in our society, which equates age with decline . . . Even further, as I discovered when I began to look into the whole question of retirement, our society exactly pinpoints the onset of that decline at age sixty-five. No one would presume to date so precisely the onset of childhood, adolescence, or adulthood, and reward— or—punish those who don't arrive or depart on time."

The phrase "betwixt and between" was first used as descriptive of the adolescent experience, hanging at the threshold of adulthood. The frustrations of struggling to grow, of floundering, or regressing, are now accepted in our understanding of the adolescent life stage. Jane Pretat, a

Jungian analyst, has also used "betwixt and between" to describe the transition experience between adulthood and old-old age. We use this phrase to identify the early post-retirement struggle of the elderescent; it catches the flavor of being caught in a space between one way of being and another, and affects a changing, evolving consciousness about oneself, one's world, and one's place in it. In her words, "The post-retirement phase also can be experienced as a time of floundering, a time when a deeper personal centering is sought. Most important—no one tells us that it might be our old way of being in the world that must die to make way for the new . . . in fright, we run off into frantic activity."

This "betwixt and between" struggle may not be apparent to some elderescents until the 'curtains are pulled back,' revealing inner turmoil that perhaps can't be avoided. Internal conflicts with a pull toward reality versus denial are voiced: "I am not old; I am still vigorous and young." "God, I can't do five sets of tennis without getting exhausted." "I have a lot still to say, but who listens? So how can I contribute?"

The struggle is in letting go of an identity that may no longer fit and in finding a new one, arousing a profound shift in one's consciousness. Kierkegaard spoke of the eternal struggle that gives further dimension to the "betwixt and between" struggle. "Whereas the life fear is anxiety at going forward, becoming an individual, the death fear is anxiety at going backward, losing individuality." This fear keeps the elderescent "to-ing and fro-ing," moving on, and regressing.

Descriptions of experimentation, toying with ideas about where to live, for example, abound in the reports of recently retired elderescents. Even five to ten years after retirement, the anxiety of this uncertainty is clear in the conversations and writings of some elderescents. For those who find new meaning and purpose in jobs or creative endeavors, this struggle abates. For some the transition period is so brief that the "betwixt and between" dynamic does not seem apparent. In the words of Pretat, "There are times when the birth of new consciousness comes suddenly in a life-changing epiphany. More often it happens slowly, preceded by a long period in which the darkness seems hopelessly black and growth of creative energy almost imperceptible," offers Pretat.

The following sections contain a sampling of personal stories from those who struggled in the early post-retirement years with difficult feelings resulting from being "neither here nor there."

"What Now?"

This poem was written by Bob Burdett, a retired accountant who is part of an elderescent writers' group similar to thousands across the United States, whose members gather to share thoughts and feelings through stories and poetry.

> Retired.
> Off the treadmill.
> Out of the rat race.
> Affairs in order.
> Paper read.
> Bills paid.
> Laundry washed and folded
> It'll only take a minute to put it away.
> Enough time for everything,
> Then some.
> Too much of a good thing.
> Too many crossword puzzles.
> Too many naps.
> Errands I used to do on the way from Point A to Point B
> have become major events.
> Is this what it's supposed to be like?
> I retired on insufficient data.
> Now I'm expected to live another twenty-five years,
> Almost 10,000 days.
> A slow death.
> Travel?
> Romantic involvement?
> Don't think so.
> Need to do something productive.
> Significant,
> Meaningful,
> Gratifying.
> Like re-invent myself:
> Start all over.

Are These Really the Golden Years?

Some retired elderescents express a patent bitterness toward the institution of retirement. For them the transition process is demoralizing.

Walter, a sixty-seven-year-old retired minister, expresses some of these feelings two years into retirement. This is a synopsis of our interview with him.

"Everyone I'm sure who has worked regularly has said, at one time or another, 'how much I look forward to retirement,' to the freedom which it will bring, the strains and tensions of life it will relieve. I am also sure that others who have voiced these words have quickly found them hollow and vain once retirement became a reality." Walter explained how he had originally confronted his congregation with his wish to retire, and how, with each of these requests, his congregation had implored him to remain. He recalls his feelings of disappointment as he relates how they eventually accepted his offer, which caused him to feel hurt and rejected. He admits his uncertainty as to whether he was experiencing internal changes that caused him to reconsider retirement or simply wanting reassurance about still being needed.

Walter remembers his mother's advice: "Never retire, for then you will quickly become nothing but a has-been. This can be particularly true for those who are alone, for those with uncertain health or for those with limited talent and personality. Often, a particular job and a certain position in life offer the main reason for being."

So much of this man's identity and sense of worth depended upon his professional role in his community that without that role he felt diminished to the point of losing his reason for being. He adds, "Of course, we all realize that sooner or later, the burden of age will make retirement necessary, indeed required, by the demands of a productive society. After thirty years in one place, I knew only too well that a different perspective, fresh ideas, new concepts, were urgently needed by my congregation. And so in this particular case my retirement seemed to be the only answer at the time."

Walter warns others against being "lulled into thinking that retirement always leads in the direction of a brighter, happier future than the past years of work have proved to be. The loss of status, a more narrow circle of good which can be accomplished, smaller financial resources; all these facts can so easily cloud the later years of life. Retirement can mean a lack of contact with the general currents of society, for days at a time, not speaking to anyone under the age of seventy." And yet, says Walter, "perhaps, just perhaps, retirement is one of the ways which Life has of preparing us all for the ringing of the Twilight Bell and then the Coming of the Dawn."

We can understand Walter's struggle as a "betwixt and between" battle, as he moves forward into uncharted territory or backward to an identity that may no longer fit. He feels a loss of individuality, and that he is of no value, a 'has been,' a castoff. In this ego struggle, in which the normally useful 'I' feels dismissed and devalued, he tries to put a more positive spin on the changes he experiences. Perhaps for him this is preparation for old age and death.

Six years later Walter was a victim of Alzheimer's disease and lived in a nursing home where he died in eighteen months.

Uncharted Ground

In yearly Christmas letters written during the first years of his retirement, John, an engineer, describes his struggle with feeling "betwixt and between."

"Well, we did it! On November 3, 1995 we both retired to explore the good life and see for ourselves if everything we have heard . . . is really true. So far, it is as good as advertised. Naturally, we are still in the 'it's just like vacation phase' as those who have gone before tell you."

John identifies three phases of the retirement process as he sees it. "The first phase is the vacation phase. One really hasn't come to realize that the long vacation-like period, will indeed, continue indefinitely and there is no Monday coming up when you will have to be at your desk.

"The second phase is the realization that this is really a new life, one dominated by an unusual level of activity that appears to be discrete rather than continuous. For example, last Monday, I did Living Classroom volunteer work in the morning, consulted in the afternoon and came home to preside at the condominium-board meeting. By anyone's count that is three separate jobs. In this phase you are interested in doing more things than time will allow. One loses the fear that one will be bored, restless, or unchallenged. I have substituted the frazzle that results from many tasks at work for that which results from many interests placing demands on my time . . . Certainly, harmony has yet to set in. We are convinced it is possible to have no free time and yet, somehow, I believe there is another phase where some settling will take place.

"Phase three could be the shedding of additional things, as one settles further into situations and associations that one favors. We went from vacation to lots of exploring to . . . I guess I found myself needing to do more mentally challenging things, which equates to work. So I started consulting. I am doing a fair amount of that here. But I feel like I'm really retired and I just dabble at work. I work for myself and I'm leisurely setting my own start and end times. I don't usually work on Monday or Friday and head off to the lake for the long weekend."

John first chose retirement because he had reached a level of employment that brought him more managerial responsibilities, taking him away from the work he really loved—engineering. He resolved some of his struggles with the "betwixt and between" phase by returning to work at a less intense pace. As an independent consultant, he was able to shed the managerial tasks, selecting projects with a technological focus, which he preferred.

A five-year spread of Christmas cards and letters from John describe the unsettledness of this early stage of elderescence. Some days he says it is satisfying and other days, frustrating.

In December 2002 John described his life as "a roll of toilet paper." "The paper always comes off the roll at the same rate, but as time goes on, the roll spins faster and faster. Sound familiar?"

Two years later we learned that John was on his way to a new full time, prestigious job and a new home across the country.

LOSS OF PROFESSIONAL IDENTITY

In 1922 G. Stanley Hall expressed his struggle with "betwixt and between" feelings after retiring: "For more than forty years I have lectured at eleven o'clock and the cessation of this function leaves a curious void . . . I am rather summarily divorced from my world, and it might seem at first as if there was little more to be said of me save to record the date of my death . . . I had moments of idealizing the leisure which retirement would bring. But when it came I was so overwhelmed and almost distracted by its completeness that I was at a loss, for a time . . . to know how to use it. But no program that I can construct seems entirely satisfactory . . . I really want and ought to do something useful and with a unitary purpose . . ."

Often the first question asked after, "What is your name?" is "What do you do?" It is the base, the root, from which much social conversation emanates. As an elderescent retiree, what do you write in the space allotted for profession/ employment when you fill out credit applications, alumnae questionnaires, etc.? *"Retired teacher? Ex-research scientist? A has-been?"*

Our culture bases its understanding of who one is by what one does, how one makes a living. Thus, one's sense of self is usually integrally connected to one's work, a self that is also influenced and shaped by the continuous and changing reflections of our world. The retiring elderescent must face this question: "Who am I without my professional identity?" Those who view the horizon as filled with opportunities for new identities and meaningful pursuits may not initially be troubled by the question; it may take time for this enthusiasm to abate, but five years into retirement the glow of hope may have dimmed.

A former senior scientist spent his first years of retirement offering his expertise to Congress and other federal institutions and agencies. He expressed optimism and enthusiasm when he first spoke of this work. Yet, five years later he reports with sadness, "there have been successes; however, there have been frustrations . . . There is resistance on the part of professional staffs to accept volunteer help because of fear of being made to appear inadequate. The internal personal competition makes the resistance unyielding. In those cases we shrug our shoulders in quietly shared acceptance and look elsewhere for the satisfaction which we want to come from useful service."

One's professional identity is not only defined by others, it is, even more importantly, how one defines oneself. Our professional and work-related identities are more than mere labels to hold onto; they are the vantage points from which we view the world, a means of focusing our attention on the things that matter, the things to which we attach great importance.

In letting go of this identity, our worlds can be shaken to the core. This confusion/ struggle between who we have been during lengthy work/ career lives and who we are in this new stage, which is still unfolding, can bring periods of feeling disoriented, empty, and lost. This "betwixt and between" struggle can consume one for years, ultimately requiring a letting go of many of our ego-driven needs.

I Have a Reputation

Ross, a retired teacher, describes issues that arose in the form of an identity crisis during the early years of his retirement. Bored and lonely at home, Ross returned to his profession only to face a loss of status and control that he found demeaning.

As a substitute teacher in an elementary classroom in a Rhode Island school Ross considered his life as he attempted to engage his restless students in a discussion. "Boy, I remember when I was a full-time teacher, I had a reputation. When students came to my class they knew what they were getting into. I never let them get away with a thing and had the support of their parents, who in many cases had been my former students. A strict disciplinarian; that was me. What happened one week when I was substituting never would have happened when I was a full-time teacher. Imagine a kid asking me why I didn't know that Halloween was over and I could take off my mask!

"I had to reestablish a pattern of discipline every time I walked back into the classroom and that kind of took the enjoyment out of it. The kids didn't know me. I didn't know them. And I didn't know where anything was. It took most of the day just to get acclimated to the set-up and then it was over. Who knew when they would call again and it was almost never in the same class again anyway . . . One day, I couldn't believe it. They called me at noon to come in, driving forty-five minutes to get there for the afternoon. I wondered if they planned to pay me literally for half a day? Twenty-five dollars before taxes for a half-day's work; that barely covered my gas expenses.

"I really thought retirement was going to be the solution. I was fifty-eight, so it seemed right. I was overwhelmed at the time. Father was rapidly declining with dementia. Mother was so weak; we had to put her in a nursing home. That really did her in. As the child living closest to them, it was my responsibility to take care of things. I really didn't have time or energy for my teaching. I had taught for thirty-two years. It had been my life, but I just couldn't cope with anything anymore. I really wasn't there for the kids anymore. That's what made me decide to retire.

"Those first few months were hell. Home alone all day. I am a verbal person. I missed the interaction. There are only so many repairs you can do on your house. Nobody to talk to. I couldn't wait for my wife to come home for dinner. I really didn't know what to do with myself. You really have to plan for retirement. You have to have meaningful things to do. There's Charlie, he's always loved golf. So he put together a business in Coventry and now he's making money and doing what he loves. He didn't really retire . . . He really just changed jobs. You need to have something to fill up the time. That's why I went back to substitute. Slowly, I guess, I picked up the pieces, making a mosaic. I imagined there would be things for me to do.

"It's been a long two years this June. The new Principal, Dr. Taylor, was hard to deal with. She had her problems; I had my own problems and couldn't take on hers. I had planned to possibly teach in Massachusetts after retiring from Rhode Island but a Superintendent there said he couldn't hire me since I had a masters degree; new graduates were financially more hirable. I said I'd take a cut in pay, but he said the union wouldn't allow it. Here I was a fifty dollar a day guy. I'm not going to do anybody any favors anymore! I ended up teaching GED classes which is challenging and enjoyable."

Nobody Calls Me Doctor Anymore

We had a chance to get to know Alice, a retired psychotherapist, one day in October in Hyannis, Massachusetts. The summer visitors had returned to their lives far from the Cape and the flurry of summer activities and distractions were gone. Life could return to normal again for those who lived here year round.

Alice was relatively new to the rhythm of seasons that comes with living in a resort community. Today she decided to venture out alone on her bicycle, taking the familiar path out of her neighborhood towards the ocean. It felt different. Was it the sudden silence after the hum of summer activities, or the fact that it had become obvious that she now really lived here year round, not just in summer?

Living by the sea had been a long-time dream. Alice and her husband had purchased a vacation house ten years ago. Then Alice had come to a point in which she wanted a simpler life, without professional responsibilities, with time to explore, meditate, and know her soul, if she had one! They made the decision to sell their home in Boston. Now, no longer was there a place to return to after vacation.

Alice related her feelings of rather mild disillusionment, in that her life seemed much the same, and, in fact, more unsettled than ever. First intrigued by the field of psychology when her family of origin had called upon the help of a psychiatrist, its various tenets had provided guidance both in her own individual therapy journey and in her work with clients for over forty years. Her work as a psychotherapist became her passion.

That afternoon Alice shared this: "I am four months into retirement. Yes, I used to know the answers. Studying Gestalt, psychoanalytic theory, and object relations, I finally brought them all together in an eclectic approach. Now what do I believe? What do I know? What do I even want? I know I had been ambitious, dedicated to success; and now I feel lost. These feelings had actually begun several years before when I had first decided to retire. The work that had once been so energizing and exciting often felt depleting. I was feeling what we call 'burn out.' Retirement seemed like a way out. It was hard leaving all my patients, the moments of intimacy and honesty, all the lives that had touched me. Then there were moments that I felt I could not listen to another person. I no longer had an answer."

As we sat and talked, Alice expressed a real sense of relief to be out of the day-to-day and hour-to-hour struggle with other peoples' problems. Then, with an obvious pang of sorrow, she said, "The life I had known is truly gone. What had it all meant? I had been in private practice so there were no public signs of departure, no company parties, no plaques acknowledging the value of one's work. Patients expressed their pain and gratitude to me in very loving ways but these were private moments. Riding by the ocean a few minutes ago I felt a wave of panic. Who am I? What do I have to hang on to? I have not only given up my work but I have given up my identity. Nobody calls me "Doctor" anymore. This is the sudden silence after the roar of work."

Alice is so obviously struggling with her sense of being "betwixt and between," and seems at an impasse. She had been so focused on her external identity that she had camouflaged her individuality and perhaps her integrity. We wanted to suggest to her that she look to herself now for answers, that she take the time to sit by the water and venture deeper into her own thoughts. A Jungian scholar once said, "When we find ourselves

. . . between one way of being and another our conscious energy is apt to disappear into the unconscious and become unavailable to us in our daily life. It is as if we fell asleep on the road to age. When this happens we may feel as if we have suddenly lost pieces of ourselves."

In a follow-up interview three years further into retirement, Alice is still uncertain about whether she needs to nurture her ego needs. Losing her identity as "Doctor" clearly caused her to feel fearful about losing her sense of self, her worth, though she may not really believe that her individuality resides in a title. In this discrepancy lies the confusion that keeps her agitated and unhappy. Alice is still uncertain about pushing forward into a new life, with all of its various and new experiences, and the opportunity to further establish her individuality along the way; she does not know if she will find enough within herself to be happy and survive. Again, Kierkegard's words seem appropriate: "Whereas the life fear is anxiety at going forward, becoming an individual, the death fear is anxiety at going backward, losing individuality."

From the Park Bench to a New Life

This next story summarizes several interviews with a thrice-retired minister who rediscovered his passion for life in returning to work.

After his first retirement, Rev. Simpkins sat alone one day on a park bench on Main Street in his hometown, seemingly waiting for something. He felt depressed, lacking in purpose, and lonely in his retirement. Seeking comfort perhaps in sharing his experience, he offered, "I have always enjoyed my ministry. Now I sit around not being employed. I face the hard question, 'What do I do now?' living alone, with no job or other significant activity to fill my days. The problem of unstructured time is still unresolved. I cook, walk the dog, watch television, sit on a park bench with friends, and lie down to rest a lot, eat sweets. All this is very unsatisfactory and does not fulfill my need to be connected, significant, and part of the active mainstream."

Each time the Reverend retired he sought new employment, first as a substance abuse counselor, then mowing lawns as Superintendent of Parks in his small community, and finally taking interim preaching jobs. His third retirement was particularly painful. "I felt that my memory was getting bad, that I was losing a sense of purpose . . . fulfillment—this retirement was quite empty and I needed to find employment."

In a conversation two years later, Rev. Simpkins revealed that he had asked the minister in charge of his area to find him another interim assignment closer to home. "I was sent to Pittsfield, Massachusetts, which is not too close . . . but I am in a small town, called Cheshire, like the cat. I am an interim pastor there. It is a troubled church; the previous minister had been asked to resign. He also had a second church about five miles down the road, called the Chapel, which he decided he would not leave. He took about half of the members away from First Baptist in Cheshire. So the congregation was in a state of shock when I arrived, upset, feeling tremendous loss, but resolving to go ahead. So here I am, a newcomer in this tiny troubled community . . ."

In talking with him the last time, Rev. Simpkins was enthusiastic, proudly relating his success at reviving this little congregation. "Their church activities had dwindled to almost nothing so I started a choir, a Women's League, and a Youth Fellowship. I have a new life. I am optimistic and delighted to be here doing this job, giving them my very best. I am seventy-two and my memory has come back. It's pretty strenuous, but I'm loving it. My morale is way boosted from the days I was sitting around on the bench on Main Street. I am happy now with myself. I am being useful and, as I say, my mental faculties are much improved."

Reverend Simpkins could not accept retirement as a viable lifestyle; for him it was deadening. Without a professional identity or tangible purpose he could not happily traverse the uncertainty brought about by such a major transition. His identity as a "good" person depended on working with and for others. By experimenting with both working and not working for several years, he had clarified his own need to work. He felt that his ministry was of value in drawing his congregation together as well as in maintaining his own sense of self and vitality.

"Didn't You Used To Be Mr. Cronkite?"

In the summer of 1999 we interviewed Walter Cronkite, who was most generous in contributing his time and thoughts in our study of the elderescent experience.

As perhaps the most esteemed communicator of critical events in our history, Walter Cronkite has been deemed, "The Most Trusted Man in America." He holds the Norman Cousins Global Governance Award presented to him by the World Federalist Association at the United Nations on October 9, 1999. With his inimitable candor he gave these remarks upon his acceptance: "I'm in a position to speak my mind and, by God, I'm going to do it! We can influence whether our planet will drift into chaos and violence or . . . whether we will achieve a world peace under a system of law."

Does this sound like a man who has retired from his life? At 82, when reflecting on the first days of his retirement from the CBS News anchor desk, Cronkite told us, "Possibly at first there was a difference, a sense of relaxation; the daily tension of breaking news stories gone, but I don't think leaving the news desk has made a major difference in my personality or my tolerance for the intolerant. I keep much busier than I intended since stepping down as anchorman and managing editor at CBS." He talked about his departure, saying that he left, "wanting more flexibility; mostly flexibility to enjoy life a little more than I was able to do with the very heavy schedule of daily broadcasting and, prior to that, the grind of daily press service work. I have been fighting deadlines my whole life."

Cronkite does assignments as a special correspondent for CBS and has produced many award-winning documentaries with his production company, The Cronkite Ward Company, formed in 1993. "My efforts continue to follow my profession but I'm able to proceed at a different pace, which is important. I'm doing documentaries and public appearances. I do not do 'lectures,' per se, but enjoy 'Conversations with Walter Cronkite,' where the format is questions and answers. I also do a great deal of writing and consulting on various projects relating to journalism and public service." With his wry touch of humor, he says, "For the past three days I keep thinking I am going to go out there (to the dock in front of his home on Martha's Vineyard) and have a swim any time now with my grandchildren. They spend most of the summer with us and they occupy a lot of my time."

With pronounced enthusiasm he supported the idea of elderesence. "Many, many people are finding whole new careers at this time in their lives. Some of them are less stressful and some of them turn out to be more so. Many turn to public service—serving as crossing guards for local schools, for example. Others launch new business careers. It is a marvelous thing, the two-career life; it can almost be an ambition in its own right: I'm going to step down from this career at fifty-five or sixty-five and do something else entirely! We can find new desires that are realized in our productive, older years."

Looking back over his life he admitted. "I can't say there's been much examination of my navel, to tell you the truth. When I read thoughts about the meaning of life I may sit back and contemplate for a while, but it doesn't occupy my frontal lobes. I do a lot of thinking but it is directed at specific objectives, like a presentation I will be making or an article I intend to write or an upcoming interview for which I will need to prepare."

Yet, when Cronkite talked about sailing and his love of the ocean, it was clear that reflection was part of his life. "We do ocean sailing which is a wonderful escape. The cellular phone can destroy that, but it hasn't destroyed it yet for me. There is an entirely different environment at sea—an essential one—that of dealing with natural phenomena. The sea and weather conditions create a whole set of demands on one and we are made much more aware of the nature around us. I derive great joy in the mere casting off of earthly bounds and getting out there on the ocean surface. Sailing has a great deal to do with the enjoyment and camaraderie of one's companions and fellow sailors. It can become a tiny universe which is the size of a boat. It is a time of reflection, particularly if you are out on the ocean as night falls. At first, I always feel a little homesickness thinking: What am I doing out here? But then I see the forces of nature and the appearance of the stars and feel the serenity of sailing at night."

Cronkite recalled an event that occurred while traveling West with his wife, Betsy, which offers their wonderful senses of humor. "You may have heard the story of the lady in Yellowstone Park last fall who came up to me and said, 'Did anyone ever tell you that you look just like Walter Cronkite before he died?' and then: 'Except, I think he was thinner.' She then turned to Betsy and said, 'Walter Cronkite is dead, isn't he?' And Betsy replied, 'Yes, I think he died of thinness!'"

The last line in Cronkite's autobiography reads, "I just hope that . . . folks will stop me . . . and ask, 'Didn't you used to be Walter Cronkite?'"

Cronkite indicated that the continual changes he faces in the years since leaving the daily anchor desk have created an unsettled feeling. In public interviews he has even said that at times he wished he had not stepped down from CBS at sixty-five. He still has much he wants to say and anticipated more exposure at CBS through the years. The avenues are more limited now though he is a frequent force and presence in television broadcast journalism and is often asked to share his observations and wonderful perspective on current events.

Part Three

The Defining Issues of Elderescence

As elderescents move past the first years of retirement, they begin to have new insights about feeling "betwixt and between." They often come to confront the deeper issues of elderescence head on. Physical aging, facing one's mortality, finding new meaning and purpose, and experiencing changes in relationships are the issues that uniquely define this period. It is a time when life's paradoxes are more visible, more evident than ever; some elderescents describe being "alive and yet dying," "full of life's desires in the weakening body," experiencing "changes and yet sameness," and "limitless imagination encased in a finite body."

This is as diverse a population as any in existence throughout the stages of life. Categorizations of any group are somewhat artificial in that generalizations about human nature are always risky. Some elderescents in their sixties will have made peace with the fact of aging and their own mortality, while others in their eighties will still be trying to compete with the young! Some will seem "wooden," clinging to their pasts, and fearful of death right up to the end.

Acknowledging the risk associated with generalization, we offer in the following pages some observations specific to elderscents in their sixties, their seventies, and their eighties. For elderescents in their sixties, particularly those who have been released from the demands and structure of their work lives, this can be a time of greater personal freedom, one that provides energy for fantasies of a new life. There may be a surge of experimentation with various ventures, which can be exhilarating, but also can result in feelings of unsettledness or of being "betwixt and between." Some in this group may choose a cautious downsizing and take on part-time work.

Elderescents in their seventies are often less inclined to need to make a "statement," or present an image than they were at sixty, and have usually settled into an acceptance of the realities of aging. Their awareness of the truth about aging, however, may precipitate a quest for greater meaning in life, and a decided shift in consciousness or looking inward.

Though it may be a time of failing energies for many, the eighties can also be a time of greater self acceptance, acknowledgment of personal change and growth, a period during which one 'wants to set the world straight, losing the self consciousness about expressing one's opinions. This can lead elderescents to make valuable contributions to their own communities and to the world-at-large.

IMAGES OF AGING

Confronting the physical part of the aging process is most often the first issue that impinges on an elderescent's consciousness. Aging is about living in time; it is a reality for us all but is not experienced as acutely until the aging process accelerates. Clear physical changes, which cannot be denied in late adulthood, can be depressing and hard to accept. For others, it becomes yet another challenge, energizing new hopes and plans.

In 1975 Robert Butler, former head of the National Institute on Aging said that we must "confront ageism and especially denial . . . redefining old and transforming the views of older persons themselves toward the aging process." Since the 1980s there has been a heightened emphasis on the "re-inclusion" of elderescents in society's mainstream, bringing new awareness of the cruelty of ageism, along with the loss of human potential, wisdom, and information. Elderescents themselves have contributed to this shift in consciousness by refusing to be "put out to pasture"—and by valuing their worth as human beings and fighting for a voice in all avenues of community life. This comes as part of an apparent shift in cultural patterns of the twenty-first century, when old people are beginning to be valued and acknowledged as resources.

In one's sixties, when the subtle signs of aging are well underway, an internal battle may ensue. At one moment these changes may be accepted and at another they may be denied. Concern about aging may become a prominent focus in one's life—a paradox that leaves one anxious—"I feel young, but I look old." How one deals with these changes can be paramount to one's well-being and survival. Some elderescents will decide to have faces lifted, eyelids raised, tummies tucked, or hair dyed. Both men and women may feel that the natural aging process will have a negative effect on their life pursuits and relationships.

In their own voices our sixty-year-old elderescents shared their appreciation of a shifting awareness of aging: "When I hit sixty, it scared me; I had always been aware of my image, concerned with looking good and the other vain ideas. So I thought I would be old . . . and therefore unacceptable."

Another confides, "I still look in the mirror and think, what's that white stuff? I would dye it but my husband won't have it. I don't want to look young, but I want to look recognizable to myself . . . I want to be able to take my face for granted to some extent."

Rose Styron admits, "My fear was that once I admitted I was sixty I would no longer be sexy, no longer a writer on the way up. I would have to think about decline and about reordering my life and changing my priorities and staying home and I don't want to do any of those things. I really think my brain is slower to process information . . . like names. Boy, is it tough. I hate to admit it."

Other sixty-year-olds combat their fears of physical aging by remaining optimistic about the present: "Sometimes when I walk by the mirror and catch the image, I see an older woman looking back. For a moment I don't realize it is actually me. Inside I always feel as though I am just beginning life. I am excited about what I'm doing now." She voices the paradox of aging, of growing old on the outside while feeling so young on the inside.

A sixty-five-year-old writer responded to the notion of being over the hill with:

" . . . rather I feel that I'm not even one-half way up . . . I am going to keep climbing strong. I am becoming me now." In anger another speaks to her concerns about aging, "By the time you get to be this age (sixty-five at the time), if you still give a flying fuck what anybody thinks about you, you're absolutely crazy . . . I don't have a fantasy of aging. Aging is one of the most foreign things ever presented to me." She continues to explain how she does not worry about her future. "To be healthy is the main thing . . . "

We can tell ourselves things that make us feel better about the aging process but ultimately we cannot deny the increasingly visible signs of the faltering body and mind. The full realization of this may come not when looking in the mirror or experiencing aches and pains after a golf game, but in quiet reflective moments alone. Then a depressing, even devastating, awareness can seem all-pervasive.

When one reaches one's seventies, some settling into the inevitability of aging may emerge. A shift in focus, toward resolving the confusing feelings about aging, has to occur to avoid becoming immobilized by depression. This requires a period of desensitization to these difficult changes, after which there is usually less vanity and angst about one's appearance and more acceptance of what is real. In reaching their seventies some people, on the other hand, become more concerned with health problems, memory loss, and image in society.

One elderescent, at the cusp of her seventieth year, speaks of, "Staying with it, allowing the total feeling to have play . . ." She tells herself, "You cannot deny it—it is happening to you and will continue. You may pay attention to diet, hygiene, cosmetic support, and the latest medical information. There is nothing you can do to avoid the decaying process." For her, reality gracefully accepted alternates with times of despair. Concluding, she says, "If I don't accept, what is the alternative . . . staying depressed, getting sick?"

Also in her seventies, an activist at the San Francisco Institute for Multiracial Justice thinks her energy level has remained much the same, though she confesses she does take a nap each day. She calls for balance in coping with aging. "Don't deny it but don't give up." Another woman in her seventies, Inge Morath, a photographer and the wife of Arthur Miller, says, "I don't think about age terribly much. I don't mind getting older; you just have to. Should I dye my hair, get a face lift?" She says, "No." Her advice on aging is, "Be yourself the best you can, because if you aren't yourself, you are nothing."

One seventy-five-year-old has a gentle thought on aging. "I relate to my aging process through my experience of nature. I don't judge things in nature. Old is not bad. Blooming is not good. It is just the natural cycle, the way things are." June Singer, a Jungian analyst and writer, talks about how she moved to Cleveland at seventy-six to incorporate the structure and support of family into her life. Moving to a new area combined with the issues of aging brought on an identity crisis. Finally, she said, "Who cares?" Her epiphany resulted in a great sense of relief.

A retired consultant in his seventies verbalizes his continuing thoughtful, ambiguous struggle. He notes his changing sense of values, his willingness to offer wisdom to the younger generations but wonders who will listen. "I am experiencing more medical problems, thanks to a lot of tennis that affected a knee, more chemicals into my body to reduce the inflammation . . . It has been said that getting older makes for greater wisdom. I like to believe that is so. But who will partake of that sagacity? We become more aware of the differences in value systems as we are out of the mainstream. Our children and four grandchildren have their own lives, their own ways of looking at life's issues . . . and as we see those differences, we wonder if that is really a sign of getting old. Are older people held in high regard in our society? The Golden Years can be easily tarnished, and it takes a lot of energy and effort to prevent this at a time when energy is lagging and when efforts are splintered into a wide variety of important and less important activities. We see a shift in how our sons react to us . . . they are starting to see us differently. They see us as old people. I'm seventy-five and my wife is seventy-two. We see more and more signs of that. And we don't like to be perceived as old people . . . even though we are. They are concerned. 'Are you sure you really ought to take that trip? Now be careful; there are an awful lot of people on the road.' We are beginning to see now the "Russian roulette" of life. When we were younger we thought, 'Yep, whatever we want to do we will be able to do. We're in control.' We realize now, that destiny, fate, whatever, has a part to play in all this. So we are in less control. From one point of view they give you some choices that you didn't have before. And if you want to sit down, read a book or write some poetry, you can do it, if that's your wish. You don't have to go to work but the Golden Years also have their surprises. The surprises are health . . . There's an inevitability to it all."

A seventy-six-year-old psychologist says, "I do look young and want to be seen as young. Psychologically I need to consider myself young . . . I have a young wife . . . Though I noticed that in gatherings we tend to talk with people more close to our own age . . . I like to talk to young people but often feel that they would prefer being around those in their own age bracket . . . I also have noticed that kids were getting up to give me their seats on the bus."

In her seventies, the actor Maureen Stapleton offers an optimistic slant about aging, "Every day is a present. I don't look forward to death by any means. I gotta give myself pep talks about trying to stay healthy and keep good spirits. I'm still eager to work . . . I think you oughta hang in for as long as you can."

Almost one hundred years ago, when formal retirement for the elderly was just becoming a fact of life, G. Stanley Hall wrote in *Senescence* the following account of his own sixties and seventies, lamenting a changing consciousness of his place in the world and touching poignantly on the despair that can come from feeling superfluous as one ages:

"In the sixties we realize that there is but one more threshold to cross before we find ourselves in the great hall of discard where most lay their burdens down and that of what remains yet to do must be done quickly. Hence this is a decade peculiarly prone to overwork. We refuse to compromise with failing powers but drive ourselves all the more because we are on the home stretch. We grow hypersensitive to every manifestation of respect or esteem and not only resist being set aside or being superseded but seek to find new kinds of service that will be recognized as useful."

"The seventies is the saddest of all birthdays and if we linger superfluous on the stage, we feel that society regards us as, to some extent, a class apart; and so we instinctively make more effort to compensate our clumsiness by spryness and gently resist the kindly offers and tokens of respect to which the young incline or, perhaps more often, are taught to render the old. . . . All our plans and efforts and prospects directed toward the future have an element of uncertainty and tentativeness. One muses about our world and what is happening to it."

These thoughts are consistent with the experiences of elderescents forced to retire throughout the first half of the twentieth century. The sadness and despair Hall describes is encountered less frequently today, though some elderescents are still plagued by feelings he referred to nearly a hundred years ago—the hypersensitivity, uncertainty, and the feeling of being obsolescent. Through open dialogue and an exchange of experiences, however, contemporary elderescents have come to appreciate that this new stage of life does have potential.

In his latest book, *Still Here*, written during his seventies after recovering from a stroke, Ram Dass relates an experience he had while traveling in India a few years earlier. "I visited the house of a dear friend who said to me, 'Oh you're looking much older!' Because I live in the United States, my first reaction was defensive . . . I thought 'Gee, I thought I was looking pretty good.'" Pausing to focus on the tone his friend used, Ram Dass then said, "I heard the respect with which he'd addressed me . . . You've done it, my friend! You've grown old! You've earned the respect due an elder now, someone we can rely on and to whom we can listen.'"

There is growing awareness that there are alternatives to the message once given to those over sixty, "Retire and Prepare to Die." A writer in her seventies presents this point of view: "It is not about staying young but about not getting old . . . Old people are invisible, young people don't see you at all. I don't mind that. One loses energy in their seventies but choosing what to do goes on."

Some elderescents ignore or deny the process of aging. The children's writer, Madeline L. Engle, writes, "I haven't had time to notice about being seventy-eight; I'm still always galloping!" At seventy-four, Liz Smith admonished, "Don't act your age, and don't give in to it."

By the time they have reached their eighties, most elderescents appear accepting of their age, proud, even, of their lengthy lives; they are more emphatic about expressing their thoughts, outspoken in their opinions, and feel deserving of a place in the world. Again we turn to G. Stanley Hall, whose thoughts about aging in his eightieth year are more positive and noble than those expressed in his sixties and seventies.

"In aging men become more judicial and giving. They see through 'shams and vanities,' have a rebirth and a curiosity for first principles, traits that can offer new possibilities for mankind . . . as faculties decline, seeing and hearing, we see ideas clearer and follow association of thought rather than those of the external world . . . if current events impress and absorb us less, we can knit up the past, present and future into a higher unity. We oldsters do see these things in a truer perspective and the time has now come to set them forth surely; senescents who have retired and enjoy a super academic freedom, have an inspiring function which they must rise to. Age, with the competence sufficient for its needs, freed from anxieties about one's future state, with none of the dangers young men feel lest they impair their future careers, should not devote itself to rest and rust or to amusements, travel, self-indulgence . . . much as the old may feel they deserve . . . these . . . but should address itself to these new tasks, realizing that it owes a debt to the world which it now vitally wants to pay . . . old age is not passive and peace loving but brings a new belligerency.

"True old age is not, as we have seen, second childhood. It is more retrospective then prospective. It looks out on the world anew and involves something like a rebirth of faculties, especially of curiosity and even of naiveté. Moreover, age is in quest of first principles just as, though far more earnestly and competently, ingenuous youth is." *(Senescence)*

In *The Measurement of My Days*, Florida Scott-Maxwell rages about the reality of being eighty and the paradox of aging, between life's longings and desires and the weakening body.

"Age puzzles me. I thought it was a quiet time. We should rest within our own confines. It may be dull, restricted, but it can be satisfying within our own walls. . . I feel most real when alone, even most alive when alone. Age defines one's boundaries. Have we got to pretend out of noblesse oblige that age is nothing, in order to encourage the others?

"My seventies were interesting and fairly serene, but my eighties are passionate. I grow more intense as I age. Being old I am out of step, troubled by my lack of concord, unable to like or understand much that I see. Feeling at variance with the times must be the essence of age. Only a few years ago I enjoyed my tranquility; now I am so disturbed by the outer world and by human quality in general that I want to put things right, as though I still owed a debt to life. I must calm down; I am far too frail to indulge in moral fervor."

When, in a 1997 speech before the United Nations he promised to speak his mind, Walter Cronkite demonstrated the passion that Florida Scott Maxwell described. In his familiar, powerful voice, Cronkite offered critical thoughts about television news today. "I thought we had pioneered television news, established some standards that would live for a while; that we had put together principles upon which television journalism would operate, and it has turned out that they didn't survive after the departure of most of us from the scene."

The famous French essayist Montaigne is purported, in his aging years, to have said, "As I get older I can speak my mind all the more." Robert Butler in *Who Survives*, suggests that perhaps another way "of describing this stage of life might be reflection and rebellion, a chance to think, to reflect on one's life, to not be encumbered by the past or by what one says now . . . to speak thoughtfully about how to better the human condition."

A number of classical and biblical stories contain references to elderescents who raged against moral inequities. Notable among them is *King Oedipus*, written by Sophocles at the age of sixty-seven, and *Oedipus at Colonus,* written when he was eighty-seven. In the latter, a Greek tragedy, a humbled Oedipus discards the passive, powerless stance he adopted in his sixties as King Oedipus, and reemerges reinvigorated at the age of eighty-seven with a renewed sense of his own power to affect his people. He learns that this "power transcends death." He confronts his son! He realizes he does matter and he can still shape events.

Outstanding elderly leaders have always made heroic contributions to their communities, changing the course of events. In one's eighties there can be a reawakening of the desire to speak out and return to the battlefield of issues and values as the elderescent realizes he *matters*. This fact needs reiterating! Elderescence is about change and loss but also about *liberation*.

Some eighty-year-olds even express joy in their aging. An elderescent dancer remarks, "I am not getting older; I am growing older. I keep developing." Another says, "Part of the wisdom of aging is that we can see what's happening, what's really going on if we are paying attention." An animal rights activist enthusiastically relates, "An aspect of aging is that I feel so much happier than I ever did. I spent my earlier years in conflict with myself . . . this has lifted . . . I live in the now . . . there is so much to do . . . our creativity gets better . . . we get knowledge."

Marion Woodman, a Jungian analyst in her eighties, offers her philosophy of aging by paraphrasing Yeats' poem *Sailing to Byzantium*.

> An aged man is but a paltry thing,
> A tattered cloak upon a stick,

unless,
Soul clap its hands and sing,
and louder sing.
For every tatter
in its mortal dress . . .

Woodman adds, "I celebrate every wound, every sacrifice, every joy, every passion, every tatter in my mortal dress," and she fights back. "I find when I travel now that some ticket agents and flight attendants pat me on the head and call me dear. That condescension irritates me . . .Well, I won't do as I'm told. They assume just because my body is frail, my mind must be, too . . . I am still in charge of my own empowerment. Now my body isn't as strong as it once was, but for all that, this fortitude that would not be conquered is still there. It refuses to be defeated."

Chronic physical problems are an undeniable struggle for some seventy-and eighty-year-old elderescents, and can become an impediment to a successful aging process. This is a challenge that needs to be confronted. Chronic health problems can rob an elderescent of much of the enthusiasm and joy possible in this stage of life.

In our interview with the past publisher of the *Washington Post,* Katharine Graham at eighty-two candidly remarked: "Aging, it is very hard. Do not make any mistake about that! Whoever said, 'Old-age is only for the brave' is absolutely correct. I mean, because I was all right until seventy-five. And after that, physically, things started to happen. It was arthritis with me but if it isn't that it's something else, you know. You can't get everything done and it takes longer. But I think you have to stay involved and stay active and above all I have tried to go on making younger friends because I had older friends, of course, but a lot of them have died. So you have to try to make younger ones as you go, which isn't that easy but it is possible if you make an effort . . . One of my best friends is my granddaughter who is thirty-three and she is absolutely marvelous."

In her autobiography, *Personal History* written in her seventies, Graham says, "I see positive aspects to being old." Yet, her response to us seven years later, in 1999, was, "Well, I think those diminish." Her response is similar to other elderescents who are living with chronic pain.

Henry P., a college professor we interviewed who is now nearing 80 years of age, spoke of what seemed a daunting undertaking carried out over the past 15 years. He successfully battled four serious health problems: coronary by-pass surgery, a serious knee injury sustained while jogging, tuberculosis, and small strokes that required carotid artery surgery. "I confronted the changes in my physical condition and have learned to live with them. I enjoy writing and at first I wrote about the family and the family events I recalled. I taught myself to play the piano keyboard and learned to play some songs before my lung condition occurred. I wrote a novel, put it aside and read it later and decided it was not very good. I wrote another and the same thing happened. Now I am writing my third and it keeps me out of 'mischief.'"

Henry has come to terms with his serious health issues, and definitely wants to continue to live, loving his family and enjoying the freedom that this time gives him. He talked fondly about "getting up when I want, making breakfast and reading the paper and then doing some chores perhaps like grocery shopping . . . I have no ambiguity about religion—it is the 'here and now' and this has become clear and comforting. But I have a lot of years yet to say 'go away reaper.'"

Another elderescent writing in *The Positive Aging Newsletter* offers his thoughts on dealing with twelve chronic illnesses. He reports having four kinds of heart disease, with a heart attack occurring at age fifty-four, as well as a seizure disorder. His philosophy, "I could let the diseases take control of my life, put a sour frown on my face, curl up in the fetal position and wait to die or I could seize control, put a smile on my face and do everything possible . . . attitude, diet, exercise, spirituality, to lead the fullest, longest, happiest life possible."

In our interview with Walter Cronkite, he spoke about his heart by-pass surgery two years prior at age 80. He admits that, "illness really shakes you up more than anything else." Until then, he had felt no diminution of physical energy, or mental ability. "I am now beginning to recognize some limitations; my endurance is not as great and I am not as flexible." He jokingly adds, "The stairs are a little steeper and the walking surfaces a little rougher."

In his poem to the young entitled *Youth, Day, Old Age and Night* (1959), Walt Whitman spoke of aging in his inimitable manner:

> Youth, Large, Lusty, Living . . .
> Youth, Full of Grace, Force, Fascination.
> Do you Know that Old Age
> May Come After You with
> Equal Grace, Force, Fascination?

Deepak Chopra, a noted exponent of the new paradigm shift in consciousness, offers words of true encouragement, declaring in *Ageless Body, Timeless Mind*, ". . . awareness has the power to change aging . . . and retaining this creative potential is the mark of non aging."

The Tao Te Ching proclaims, "Whatever is flexible and flowing will tend to grow; whatever is rigid and blocked will wither and die."

Robert Butler, author, and former Head of the National Institute on Aging suggests that many of the unpleasant stereotypes of aging are really a result of disease, discrimination, and pre-aging personality characteristics, a further indication of a shift in our understanding of aging. Aging may be mutable!

One of the most touted myths supported by social scientists for decades assumed that one's abilities and creative processes begin to deteriorate at mid life,—in the forties and fifties. This is often the justification supporting widespread cultural ageism. Stories of elderescents whose creative abilities are recognizable as they live into their eighties defy this stereotype.

In the 1970s psychologists began to investigate the ingrained belief that learning and memory capacities decrease with age. Advances in the methodology of these investigations substantiate the fact that memory and certain learning skills do change with normal aging. The type of materials and tasks scored in these studies, however, bias the changes measured.

Other studies found that older people learn and remember those things that are of interest to them, filtering out the trivial. "The changes are a product of their life experiences. Moreover, their recollections are more distilled and more reduced to primary material than those of young people." Two studies, one done at Columbia University and the other at Duke University, found no decline in I. Q. in subjects sixty-five to seventy-five years old. Linear thinking misrepresents the changes that time brings to functioning. The elderescent mind can maintain flexibility for higher states of awareness that the younger mind may not. (cited in *Seasons of Life*)

Dr. Gene Cohen, a psychiatrist turned gerontologist and a "game maker," has created a Center for Aging in Washington, DC, where he studies creativity in the older population. "We've grossly misunderstood the potential for creativity in the older life," he writes. "A lot of these folks know who they are and have time to pursue these things."

He suggests that creative energy promotes better health, positive emotions, and a better functioning immune system. His research posits that "there is actually an increase in the length and extent of dendrite branching connecting brain cells" from one's fifties to late seventies.

Dr. Warner Schale, a professor from Penn State University cited in *Seasons of Life*, spent thirty years studying aging and says, the mental decline he saw, he believed, was "unnecessary. "The idea that your mind goes down the tubes is nothing more than a myth, but it can be self-fulfilling. Once people leave the work world they let their intellectual skills drop, unless they get a second job, volunteer, or learn new skills. Decline can be reversed," he claims.

Throughout the ages, a few remarkable elderescents have proved that they can provide the world of science, literature, politics, music, and art with extraordinary contributions. It is hardly necessary to debate this point. But for impressions' sake we can cite several examples. Michelangelo designed St. Peter's Basilica in Rome during a sixteen-year period when he was between the ages of seventy-two to eighty-eight. Plato's *Dialogues* were written when he was an old man. Galileo completed *Dialogue Concerning Two New Sciences* at the age of seventy-four. Antonio Stradivari built the famous Habeneck and Muntz violins in his nineties. Mary Baker Eddy founded the Christian Science Monitor at the age of eighty-seven. Frank Lloyd Wright designed the Guggenheim Museum of Art in New York City at the age of ninety-one. Mahatma Gandhi achieved India's Independence from the British at the age of seventy-seven. Picasso, Golda Meir, and Dr. Seuss all achieved their greatest accomplishments in their seventies, eighties, and nineties.

We can also cite contemporary elderescents renowned for their great achievements: Walter Cronkite, John Glenn, Lee Iaccoco, Katharine Graham (recently deceased), Hugh Downs, Jimmy Carter, Colin Powell, and Mike Wallace, to name a few, as well as many special elderescents that we have interviewed for this book.

In *The Courage to Grow Old,* an impressive collection of stories edited by Phillip Berman, 41 prominent men and women reflect on growing old while still actively contributing to society. We have included a few examples from this collection that reflect the changing consciousness about aging and the astounding wisdom and appreciation of life exhibited by these men and women.

Margaret Coit Elwell, born in 1919, remains one of our country's foremost biographers. In 1985, she received a Pulitzer Prize for a biography of John Calhoun. "It would be comforting to those seeking the courage to grow old to think that ageism is gone now," she laments, "but ageism is for the aged to find the courage to conquer . . . what if Picasso or Pablo Casals or Michelangelo had been put to sleep in their seventies, we would have missed their great art in their eighties and nineties . . . Where do we find the courage to grow old? We find it in the good fight! By fighting the battles."

Jules Olitski, a painter in his late seventies, says that his goal in life is delight. When he feels he lacks courage or is afraid to try new experiences, he tells himself he could die at any moment. This notion frees him. "I have nothing to lose."

At eighty, Enola Maxwell, executive director of a community agency, offers hope, "I don't have very much time to sit back and be old, because there's still so much undone. I tell old people, too, that we have to be the ones now to get in front of the bulldozers—we should not leave it to the young people . . . stop resting and get up and help others . . . there's no sense in resting, you've got eternity to rest . . . no sense retreating now. We have to be the ones now to get out in front."

FACING MORTALITY

Elderescents are the ones most qualified of any group to share soberly and eloquently the ways in which they face their own mortality. We are all on a journey without a known timetable but all have as the final destination death. Because death is more apt to occur in elderescence, or in the old, old stage of senescence, it is more imperative that one deal honestly and directly with this inescapable event. As many elderescents emphasize, until one truly faces and accepts the reality of death one cannot rest. Whether we accept death as final or believe that there is life after death, we must accept the eventuality of our own mortality before we can get on with the remainder of our lives.

Mortality is an issue we rarely talk about until we reach elderescence. It can become a central source of anxiety and dread that can throw one into a 'betwixt and between' struggle, between life and death, requiring time to come to terms with its inevitability. It can be a paradox that one has difficulty living with. In T. S. Eliot's poem, *The Love Song of J. Alfred Prufrock*, we hear Prufrock speaking vividly about his own death.

> I grow old . . . I grow old . . .
> I shall wear the bottoms of my trousers rolled . . .
> I have seen the moment of my greatness flicker.
> I have seen the eternal footman hold my coat, and snicker.
> And in short, I was afraid.

The loss of a future, now more imminent than at any other stage, may be *the crisis* of elderescence; retirement may be the point at which many elderescents first begin to face their mortality. Letting go of one's professional identity may be seen as the last great transition before dying, and is surely the deep-seated fear underlying the identity crisis that often follows retirement. "Who am I now?" "Do I exist?" These questions are motivated by the consciously acknowledged or unconscious thought that death is "just around the corner." It can be an awakening! In the early 1900s retirement often meant death *was* "just around the corner!!"

In Robert Butler's book *Why Survive?*, he speaks about accepting death: ". . . when it does come, it may eventually be preceded by a gentle, predictable decline. Sensitivity to the psychological meaning of death will contribute toward making the last crisis of the life cycle a time for potential meaning and summation. We actually have within our grasp the chance to live the gift of life fully and completely up to the moment of death itself."

Aging can be experienced as a narcissistic injury. The challenge may begin when the first physical signs of aging trigger our initial fears about the nearness of death.

Letting go of the belief in the permanence and uniqueness of our individual selves can be extremely difficult. While many elderescents in their sixties claim their decisions to retire were the result of personal choice, the factors affecting these decisions may be related to concerns arising from a medical crisis, raising concerns about their own mortality. Cancer, a heart condition, or even simply a decrease in energy level becomes motive enough to leave a job.

A retired elderescent professor explains, "In my case there were a couple of factors that led me to think about retirement. One of which was I discovered I had atrial fibrillation. I then started thinking about my mortality . . . even more than I did during World War-II. I started thinking how many more years do I have left and what do I want to do?"

Two years later, realizing he had lost interest in his teaching, he decided, "It's time for me to move on." The lessening of interest in one's profession is often the first mark of transition into this new stage of life. "The university gave me the golden handshake and I was on my way." Yes, and on his way to a new passion, learning and playing jazz as a professional musician at the age of sixty-eight. Two factors, recognition of his own mortality and a desire for change, encouraged him to look at his future, leave behind a work life that no longer fit, and set off in a new direction entirely.

Arthur, a psychologist, confronted mortality early in his career when his daughter died of leukemia at age sixteen. His own father died at the age of fifty-nine from coronary heart disease. "It was really funny for both my brother and me, the year that we were fifty-nine, we kind of stood around waiting for something to happen. I think my view of pursuing interests in life changed because of these two events . . . if I wanted to do something I jolly well better get on with it. My father's death at fifty-nine and hearing him always planning to retire at some point influenced my push toward my own retirement. If you put some of these things off too long, you may not get a chance to do them. Looking at people that do not successfully retire, I think that one factor may very well be their lack of acceptance of their own mortality. A friend called a couple of years ago and wanted to go out to dinner to talk. He has not retired but he keeps trying to and failing at it, going back to work. He had never really considered that he might die until his brother died, and that was probably a factor in why he found it difficult to retire because that meant he was closer to dying. He could not accept his own mortality."

Roszak, author of *America The Wise*, speaks of his own health crisis in his sixties and his survival by a medical miracle. Although this did not lead directly to his retirement, it was the "decisive point at which I moved beyond the follies of senior life into wisdom." To make the best use of that kind of experience, he says, "We may need professional guidance to achieve an awakening into an authentic rite of passage."

Cronkite shares a similar experience to that of Roszak, "I don't think I even blinked over mortality before my heart surgery, but since then I have an appreciation that immortality has not been visited upon me exactly."

Even without a medical crisis, anxiety about one's mortality may begin to enter one's consciousness in the seventh decade of life. As we see from the following excerpts, people in their seventies often begin adopting different attitudes. "As you realize the number count is getting short," says one person, "it can lead to a lot of anxiety and it can also allow you to take a longer view and try to get things in proportion. It is difficult."

A dancer in her sixties speaks about growing older and living with the idea of impermanence as an attempt to accept the inevitability of death. Her experiences in India, where she happily adopted the idea of *growing* older, not getting older, had a substantial affect on her. "Aging is the progression of time . . . it is inevitable. I am very aware that death is there and we live surrounded by that knowledge. The nature of life is impermanence."

In one's seventies, the second phase of elderescence, concern for one's mortality may take the form of 'putting one's house in order' as a way of deflecting the fear of death and giving one a sense of control. However, once one's personal affairs (wills, etc.) are in order, lending these activities a sense of closure, some people in this stage may be more willing to reflect on their fear of death in terms of the real loss of a future.

Many have accepted that the old way of being in the world must die. This can be a moment of a deep shift in consciousness, and an awareness of entering a new stage of life. In her seventieth year, Betty Friedan comments, ". . . success now is staying alive." (*Fountain of Age*) Focusing on the present, not the future, has been her comfort.

Ram Dass (*Still Here*) speaks of handling the denial of dying. "Be aware of all of nature's process of dying, decay and feelings of disgust . . . watch your feelings, meditating on decay so you can find the place in you that has nothing to do with that. Opening to all those feelings . . . because denial of them keeps you stuck in the fear."

Just prior to his seventieth birthday, Jung suffered a severe heart attack. At sixty-seven he had written, "I can scarcely keep pace and must watch out that the creative forces do not chase me round the universe at a gallop . . . I have to coax myself soothingly, with great attentiveness not to do too much." Three years later, after recovering from the heart attack, he wrote, "The vision of the end of all things gave me the courage to undertake new formulations, surrender myself to the current of my own thoughts . . . an unconditional yes to that which is." He believed that his new thoughts came not from the ego but from a deeper source, the archetypal wisdom of the ages.

We have found that in one's eighties there is a greater acknowledgment of the uncertainties of one's future. Again, from Florida Scott-Maxwell, who speaks poignantly of dealing with death in *Measurement of My Days*: "Only with friends of my own age we can cheerfully exchange the worst symptoms and our black dreads as well. We frequently talk of death for we are very alert to the experiences of the unknown that may be so near and it is only to those of one's own age that one can speak frankly."

In reaching her eighties, Katharine Graham also spoke of the uncertainty of her future: "You inevitably think something about how you are going to die. Will it be quick which one hopes, or painful which one hopes not. I have morbid thoughts, you know, when I say, 'I'll see you next year.' I always privately wonder if I will. Well, half the time you sort of look at it the way you always have and half the time you're more realistic. Obviously I don't think about what I will do in ten years."

After his heart surgery, Walter Cronkite offered, "It is very hard to think seriously about the future, the future fades into a kind of miasma I find difficult to penetrate. And the ability to get excited about what's going to be happening in 2010 has lost some of its edge."

Rabbi Shalom-Schacter Zalman, founder of the Spiritual Eldering Project, as well as a mystic and theologian, stresses the need for elderescents to face death if they are to live with dignity. He believes that mortality must be confronted in earnest in elderescence; not long after the first awareness of the aging process begins, he says, the shadow of mortality appears. Even when someone says, "death is part of life and I take it in my stride," that individual has noted it and called it to his attention.

Some elderescents seem to take a fatalistic position on the issue of death: "When you die, you are dead and that is it. Other times," says this elder, "I am all over the place—fearful and then accepting. I do not believe in a hereafter . . . when we die, we die–that's resolved."

Others express denial of concerns about death: "I am immortal (laughs). I am sure something is going to happen to me and then I will have to face it. If I go . . . or if I stay, death is part of life . . . I am in the here and now."

Another says, "I am non religious. I went to a college reunion and hearing of colleagues who had died made me aware . . . that is very upsetting, that's worrisome, but I guess I haven't really dealt with the issue of death. I have no religious connection, though I have an interest in things humanistic and spiritual . . . I live to be active."

From a seventy-eight-year-old elderescent: "My mortality doesn't grip me . . . not too alarming . . . though maybe I am in denial. My wife thinks I am. I am not into looking at it . . . it's there and I will live with it . . . no immediate pressures on me to think about it." Though he came from a very religious family, he left the faith when he met an atheist in the Navy. "There is no beautiful place to go when we die."

Fear of death often lessens in eighty-year-olds, when there is no unfinished business. We may hear the refrain, "I have nothing more I need to do or accomplish." An eighty-two-year-old author told us, "Dying would be nice . . . just published a book and have lived a full life."

Soron Kierkegaard in *Fear and Trembling* advised, "We cannot escape the dread of death." He stated, "In becoming human, our consciousness creates the dread, the anxiety regarding non being . . . While each of us has an identity that transcends the natural order of species survival, never can we transcend our personal demise. This dualism of the human condition is the price we must pay for being human." Kierkegaard offered an interesting paradox, "limitless imagination encased in a finite body . . . ultimately this duality collapses into material nullity." He dropped dead one day on his way back from his publisher, never to reach his time in aging when an acceptance of his own death might have been experienced.

There is a definite transitional shift in consciousness around the issue of death that is unique to elderescence. In early elderescence aging is finally acknowledged. In later elderescence a de-sensitization to the ego demands is, hopefully, achieved and with this death is accepted. Elderescents in their later years shared with us this final acceptance, as in: "Death is a positive phase in my development cycle rather than the ultimate disaster of our dominant culture. Death is a part of life and I take it in my stride. Living life in fear of death is losing it. Life is impermanent and death is inevitable."

From a Buddhist perspective the beginning of wisdom for Gotama the Prince was exposure to the infirmities of old age and death. Through this confrontation with impermanence, he saw the truth of suffering and its cause in the craving for permanence. An antidote, a way of dealing with the fear of death and the unknown, is to think about a spiritual life, to think of something greater than oneself that transcends time. Another antidote is to simply appreciate living in the moment.

For many it is the dying *process* itself that is of concern: "Death is a peaceful image. I have had a full life . . . I don't want to end in a nursing home, though."

"We go to ashes . . . there are memories . . . there is the genetic left over and the genes," says one elderescent, while another says she is not concerned about death "but the dying process, of possibly long-term nursing care, loss of independence, a diminished world."

Today the horror of dying brings images of a prolonged life in a nursing home, feeding tubes, and loss of control over how one dies due to 'progress' in the field of medical technology and drugs. Perhaps the elderescent population, after coming to terms with death as a natural end to living on earth, will educate those who follow about death with dignity.

For elderescents with a religious affiliation and for those who view life within a spiritual context, mortality engenders less anxiety. Their faith provides them with a sense of death as a heavenly retreat, a guided journey, another kind of existence in an afterlife. Death is for the body only, not for the soul.

Most great religions have offered the promise of life after death, for the followers, the possibility of a future existence. Jung spoke, in *Stages of Life* about holding the belief in an afterlife as good 'psychic hygiene,' though he acknowledged that there seemed to be no scientific justification for it. "From the standpoint of psychotherapy it would therefore be desirable to think of death as only a transition, as part of a life process whose extent and duration are beyond our knowledge."

The question of immortality can only be answered by faith. However, in the realm of spirituality, there has been a decided shift in hopes and beliefs about the reality of an afterlife. There seems to be a new surge of hope in possible evidence of soul travel after it leaves the body, with new and more credible scientific research to support these findings.

Elderescents, because they must grapple with death and all that it entails—acceptance of who they are and who they have not been and the resolution of other unfinished business—can speak to us about death and dying. They can help us understand the concept of death, share their sensations, fears, dreams, and wisdom. And yet, ultimately, it will be each individual's inner journey, one of reflection, review, and search for meaning that will help to find peace in dying. This is an arena in which elderescents can offer their experience and wisdom. The subjects of death and dying have received some attention, but hopefully this will increase as elderescents share their wisdom.

Do we want immortality? Is the answer to be found in the theory offered by Erik Erickson, that we can find immortality in *generativity*, that we live on in the lives of our children and grandchildren? More recently the concept of generativity has been extended to include the notion of living on after physical death in our artistic endeavors, our written words, political actions, and our great deeds rendered on behalf of humanity. In the words of Dr. Ernie, "When my neurotic need to achieve rears its head, I drive past the Center and look at my name (Zimbelman) on the building that will be there long after I am dead. This is a monument that tells me I don't have to prove anything more. I have a legacy."

Arthur, referred to previously offers an interesting perspective on immortality. "To retire successfully, I think you have to look upon living your life as the purpose! I no longer have anything to prove. If anyone wants to know about me they can look me up in *Who's Who in America!* So now I can go and do things as the spirit moves me. I tell people I am an explorer. Remember the comic strip Calvin and Hobbes. I am like Calvin talking to Hobbes and telling him about the world out there, 'Come on Hobbes, old buddy, let's go exploring.' That's the way I look at my living my life. I used to say, 'If you survive the day, you have been successful, then everything else on top of that is frosting on the cake.' I think we have lost the concept that success is our own survival." Does he have the definitive perspective on immortality?

One's realization that control over life is an illusion is often first confronted in elderescence. The belief that we control our destinies, can have what we want, and succeed if we try hard enough, is so much a part of the human psyche. We see it operating in the infant screaming to be fed, attended to, or held, demanding that its needs will be served. Immediately there is an interplay; who is in control? As the child begins to appreciate that the adult world may not always comply with satisfying his or her needs, the child may attempt to deal with its disappointments by seeking control over how he lets those in his world affect him. The child, the adolescent, and the young adult, on the other hand, will have to modify those behaviors that are unacceptable in society at large.

As Judith Viorst explains in her book *Imperfect Control,* the development of our sense of who we are is greatly influenced by how we have experienced control issues. Her thesis states that we all have to accept the fact that control is always imperfect, is an illusion. Many of us, throughout our adulthood, have operated under the illusion that somehow, somewhere, we can achieve a dreamed-of existence, a new relationship that will better meet our needs, a place to live that will offer more of nature's joys, the perfect job that will enable us to 'climb the ladder of success,' which we so deserve, etc.

"We continue to believe in our freedom to get where we're going, to be what we strive to be," says Viorst. "Possessed of a view of an infinitely flexible, fixable self, a self unconstrained by fate or destiny; we place our trust in personal control."

The idea that, at best, control is imperfect does not impress or impede our fantasies of success. One elderescent so clearly confronted this sense of loss of the illusion of control after a committee meeting in an organization in which she had been very influential. The incident was not profound, but the reverie about it was illuminating as she shared her story: "As I reviewed and reflected upon my changing position in the board meeting last night, I experienced a profound sense of loss of control in effecting what I believed should be done. I was not angry; I was jolted by a new reality. I grew up with the admonition that, 'Where there is a will, there is a way.' I had believed that about myself. I had not operated under the belief that I would always get what I thought I wanted at any moment in time. I had experienced many failures and setbacks, but I had over time been able to retrace, change gears, and revise my wants.

"This time the felt-experience was so different. Yes, I would have to revise my sense of my role, and what I could affect. However, there was a clear urgency to look at the experience, the reality of my changing power to achieve influence in the peopled external world. The younger generation was in the driver's seat suddenly and I could see that reality. They had come in with new enthusiasm, new ideas, new energy, and their own agenda. They did not have all the answers; but they believed in their power to make things happen,—as *we* had once believed. The elderescents' orchestration of the direction of the group was over. I wanted to stay with the process, and from a more detached position could offer wisdom. Stepping back from the front lines enabled me to view clearly the new directions that the group was taking, seeing a comprehensive overview I could not have entertained if I was still embroiled in the active process."

Released from the illusion of control, this person was able to observe the ebbs and flows of change, and the reality of impermanence. The *loss of the illusion of control* must be faced with honesty and acceptance in this new stage of life. It would be hard to deny we lose control over our bodies as they age; our roles change dramatically, and our sense of ourselves demands revisiting. As we face our mortality, we cannot change the inevitability of death.

Is the ultimate control over one's death suicide? Socrates took hemlock when facing a death sentence. In England the Hemlock Society was created to assist victims of incurable diseases to die according to their own time schedules.

More recently, "rational suicide," until now little documented, is engendering more discussion. Dr Bruno Bettelheim, for example, a noted elderescent psychologist who was not suffering from a terminal illness, ended his life by committing suicide. Carol Heilbrun, retired professor of literature from Columbia University, also committed suicide, which the *Washington Post* reported as a "rational suicide." (summer of 2003) She was not purported to be in ill health or depressed; her suicide was apparently the act of a sane woman who chose to die at the age of seventy-seven.

In her book, *The Gift of Time,* written when Heilbrun was seventy-one, she described retirement as joyful, and free from feelings of anger. She had moved to a new home and was enjoying her writing. She also wrote in *Gift of Time* that life after 70 could "be dangerous, lest we live past both the right point and our chance to die." Might she have experienced some premonitions of impending decline? In the July 2003 issue of *Women's Review of Books* she wrote, "living with uncertainty that there was no further work demanding to be done" made her feel she was living on borrowed time. Her suicide note read, "The journey is over. Love to all."

Margaret Battin, professor of philosophy at the University of Utah, writing on rational suicide, states that this "represents one of the fullest forms of expression of one's autonomy. It is the right of people to shape the ends of their lives." Rational suicide will undoubtedly become a matter of greater concern as people are living into their eighties and nineties, particularly if they are unable to continue to find purpose, fulfillment, and joy in their new pursuits. Bettelheim and Heilbrun were no longer able to realize meaning and purpose for their lives. Confronting their loss of the 'illusion' of control at this stage of life, neither wanted to continue struggling to accept the true uncertainty of their situations.

MEANING

"After one has lived a life of meaning, death may lose much of its terror. For what we fear most is not really death but a meaningless and absurd life." (Robert Butler)

As we have noted earlier, the greatest assault on older workers was forced retirement, institutionalized in our country throughout the first half of the twentieth century. The admonitions— 'Retreat, retire, you are obsolete', resulted in loss of status and power, and, most importantly for many, created a void of meaning in their lives.

One hundred years later, we are able to examine the legacy of the marginalization of elderescents, and to study longevity, and the hope it affords us all, with greater understanding. A shift in consciousness has brought us away from the belief that aging is essentially a deterioration in thought and wisdom, a time in which to simply wait for death. We have moved toward the determined acknowledgment that all elderescents have critical gifts to offer and journeys to take in answering the question, "Who am I now?" For elderescents who are willing to step back and acknowledge the external and internal changes that come with aging, a need to revisit one's purpose in life will become apparent. It may be the most profound experience one can have in moving from adulthood to elderescence.

A preliminary exploration of this search for meaning may begin with 'what is meaning'? Meaning is the significance and understanding of concepts. Personal significance gives meaning to life. Ultimate meaning may be elusive. Religious ideology can offer ultimate meanings, but one has to accept the belief system with faith in order to accept the answers to one's questions as truth.

Human institutions create meaning; societies create meaning; culture gives meaning. Making myths is a way of portraying meaning. Cultures and religions explain the creation of life and even the purpose of life through myths, encouraging individuals to accept these images, thus connecting them to their larger communities. Many religions also offer explanations as to how the world began, while science proposes various concepts and theories about our universe from its observations and from the interpretation and manipulation of information. Political and social values derived from the secular world may also be the foundation for a belief system that gives one meaning. And, lastly, psychologists offer meaning through self-knowledge.

The search for meaning is a personal journey, an integral part of the process in seeking to find and know one's *essential* self, and who that self becomes near the end of one's life.

There are many ways that people try to put meaning into their lives. Meaning can come through connectedness to community, family, and friends. Tasks can provide one with temporary meaning, activities offer focus, and educational pursuits can give import to one's life. Yet, meaning that gives one a reason for existence ultimately must come through one's own internal journey. In the words of the renowned psychiatrist, Victor Frankl, "Man's search for meaning is the primary motivation in his life. This meaning is unique and specific in that it must and can be fulfilled by him alone: only then does it achieve a significance which will satisfy his own will to meaning." (*Man's Search for Meaning*)

Meaning is so essentially a part of human existence. Yet, until recently, the general population sadly has overlooked the fact that profound shifts in meaning occur with the aging process. Looking back again to the writings of G. Stanley Hall we appreciate his foresight in spelling out the need to find one's authentic self as one goes through the aging process, and in relinquishing the need to act younger than one is, or, conversely, frail and infirm. The need is for elderescents to "construct a new self just as we had to do at adolescence, a self that both adds to and subtracts much from the old personality of our prime." *(Senescence)*

Today more scholars like Lars Tornstam are suggesting "in aging, meaning may come from a new 'meta world' paradigm, where values, needs, sense of reality, and sense of self evolves." It is a fallacy to think of elderescence as simply a continuation of the patterns, values, and definitions of adulthood. Jung also spoke to this fallacy as a tragedy. He declared that the meaning and tasks of old age must be appreciated as quite different.

Self-Knowledge

Today, we can accept the concept that the primary task in aging is to become acquainted with one's personal self, one's personal meaning, one's one-and-only self. Personal reflection and meditation, religious study, and reflection are paths people take to achieve this task. A spiritual journey or a personal crisis can often awaken one to new meaning, as can a personal psychotherapy journey. The essential element is that individual meaning comes from within. If this does not happen in elderescence, despair will certainly cloud the aging process.

Victor Frankl, in his description of his survival in the German concentration camps during World War II, emphasizes that, for himself and for others who lived through the camps, survival depended on a daily focus, on a personal, concrete life *meaning* despite the unbearable circumstances. This differed for each individual, he said, and would change from day to day. What matters is that an individual person's life has specific meaning.

Frankl speaks of this as creating inner tension. The 'betwixt and between' feelings described by many elderescents when faced with unstructured time and empty space may be an expression of this struggle to find new meaning. Frankl notes that in the Nazi concentration camps those who survived were those who assumed tasks to fulfill. "Each of us can only answer for our own lives . . . to life he can only respond by being responsible."

So much of the external structure of life changes for the individual as he/she transitions into elderescence. Initially life seems unstructured, lacking in goals, free but open-ended and uncertain.

Freedom From Perfection

One elderescent we interviewed epitomizes this struggle with inconsistencies in his changing sense of self. When he remains conscious about his changing self, life begins to take on new meaning.

At sixty-five John G. took a "buyout." He describes his struggle, during an initial four-year period into his retirement, to achieve a sense of the freedom he had wished for in retirement. "I desired to do other things . . . to have freedom to choose . . . But too much freedom results in a lot of wasting of time. I don't remember which analyst wrote *Escape from Freedom*, but I believe I understand the concept better now."

Retirement created a vacuum in the structure provided by work. John did not want to give up his freedom, thus it was hard for him to seek new external structure. He acknowledges that he is a poor self-manager; however, he understood that ordering his life could bring a sense of meaning and purpose. His strong work ethic and the need to be of service to others conflicted with his wish for freedom!

"That is probably the most meaningful issue I have to cope with now," he comments. In reflecting on this dilemma, he sees that his commitment to excellence, his ego's need to excel, impinges on his desire for unbounded freedom. John has experienced the "freedom *from*"—and the release *from*—work demands, but cannot allow the "freedom *to*" phase to begin, in which one's creative dreams can be real.

Seeking meaning consistent with one's new life stage is an important step for the emerging elderescent. Old beliefs, attitudes, and the driving forces of adulthood have to be confronted. John's story is symbolic of many elderescents. In his effort to achieve a state that feels free, he fights the progression into individuality out of fear of losing the status and identity he's worked to acquire. If he gives up his ideal of perfection then he gives up what previously gave him meaning. Perfection as a central meaning in life has left him in a state of anxious paradox!

The transition to new beliefs requires reflecting on, maybe grieving for, what he must leave behind, allowing inner wisdom from his deep sense of self to surface, to come to his rescue

Fromm's prescription for meaning through genuine freedom: "spontaneous activity, and love and work which will unite man again with the world"—would require that John relinquish his belief in perfection. It would allow him to launch the journey to bring new meaning to his elderescent life, meaning that is more consistent with his new feelings and desires.

Finding new meaning may take time, as Jung notes in *Stages of Life*, "Thoroughly unprepared we take the step into the afternoon of life, worse still, we take this step with the false assumption that our truths and ideals will serve us as hitherto. But we cannot live the afternoon of life according to the programme of life's morning: for what was great in the morning will be little at evening, and what in the morning was true will at evening have become a lie." Jung had projected the emergence of human longevity in the 1950s but suggested that mankind would not reach its seventies and eighties without a reason for existence. "The afternoon of human life must also have significance of its own and cannot be merely a pitiful appendage of life's morning . . . Whoever carries over into the afternoon the law of the morning . . . must pay for it with damage to his soul."

As precious as the values of adulthood may seem, establishing a career, home, and family, these goals are no longer viable in elderescence. Jung continues, "Restlessness begets meaninglessness and the lack of meaning in life is a soul sickness whose full extent and full import our age has not yet begun to comprehend."

Elderescents must go back to the 'drawing board:' they must search for new meaning and the purpose life holds for them now.

In *New Passages* Sheehy offers, "the search for meaning . . . becomes the universal preoccupation of the second adulthood (which we call *elderescence*). It could be called the meaning crisis. It is based on a spiritual imperative: the wish to integrate the disparate aspects of ourselves, the hunger for wholeness, the need to know the truth."

Meaning signifies an underlying essence, an *isness*. It is an element of *being*. In the words of Nietzsche, "He who has a why to live for can bear almost any how . . . "

Without a foundation in meaning elderescents may become mired in confusion and anxiety, as they meander aimless and disorientated in the "betwixt and between" struggle. They may try to fill the void in meaning by doing: reading, experimenting with escapes such as alcohol or other drugs, considering new hobbies, taking trips, buying a new house, running for office, or part-time work.

In the words of Camus, "There is but one truly serious problem and that is . . . judging whether life is or is not worth living."

When the time clock stops, it's up to the retiree to make a new life, one with joy and meaning. Undeniably, many do not make the transition. Suicide statistics for the elderescent group are staggering. A 1990 report from the Center for Disease Control in Atlanta declared that the elderly as a group had the highest suicide rate in this country. Twenty-five percent of those who commit suicide are sixty-five and older, though they represent only thirteen percent of the total population.

Experiencing life without meaning and purpose, and seeing themselves as burdens, elderescents may find life not worth living. As was mentioned in Part Two, Carol Heilbrun, professor and author, who spoke so beautifully in *Gift of Time* about the sense of freedom in retirement, committed suicide at the age of 77, though she was not ill. She wrote that, after seventy, one should have the choice of whether or not to continue living. Had she lost a personal meaning for her life?

Alcoholism also presents us with frightening statistics. The American Medical Association calls alcoholism the hidden disease of people over sixty. Alcoholism for this age group has been reported at levels as high as 68 percent. A counselor at one alcohol treatment center recently declared it is so widespread that what we see is 'only the tip of the iceberg.' When work lives end, many people flounder and feel lost. Bored, with few internal resources, and often without meaning and purpose, many elderescents reach for relief "in the bottle." Lack of accountability leaves them free, but if there is no internal 'director,' a source for meaning, then life can become pointless. "A perpetual holiday is a working definition of hell," said George Bernard Shaw.

The following account illustrates how one elderescent became seduced by alcohol.

"I retired from a pressured job. I was happy to retire. I looked forward to playing golf, traveling, and spending time just relaxing. After a round of golf I'd have a few drinks with my partners. In the evening my wife and I would go out to dinner with friends and have more drinks. Then when I felt at loose ends, uncertain as to what to do next, I'd resolve the conflict with a drink. The drinking began earlier and earlier. I was only accountable to myself now. Life began to feel empty with no meaning. I was drifting . . . and I would drink to relieve the loss of meaning and little sense of self."

Eventually a family intervention helped this man face his rapid decline. In treatment he was able to assess what he'd lost through retirement and alcoholism. He realized that he needed to find a new 'something' that gripped his heart and soul, making him eager to get up in the morning. Reclaiming some of his own values and reflecting on his natural abilities, he began to regain his self-worth and to seek new meaning in his life. He is now a counselor at an alcohol treatment center, and writes about his personal journey into despair. Ralph Waldo Emerson's comment is pertinent here: "A task is a life preserver. The purpose chosen will reflect the *meaning of life* that resides in the depths of our sense of our being."

When elderescents reach their seventies they have generally accepted that the competitive ego-driven, frantic activities of their sixties must give way to an accommodation and acceptance of one's changing energies, feelings, and values.

"The death we shiver against in the wee hours could be symbolic or even a new beginning," suggests psychoanalyst Jane Pretat. "This is the struggle of the transition when the outer activities of the world lose their fascination and the inner world of the (elderescent) needs attending." Socrates, who was perhaps the first psychotherapist, is best known for his statement, "Know thyself: the unexamined life is not worth living. Keep asking questions as long as you live, for in a democracy it is essential that people think for themselves." Facing his own execution, he boldly declared, "I will not stop questioning."

The quest for a personal meaning that provides purpose for life may be the task that sustains reflection and self-examination *throughout* elderescence. As Frankl determined, meaning arises from a uniquely individual sense of self. And, in the words of the physicist David Bohm, meaning has intention. "Without meaning there could be no consciousness . . . we are the totality of our meaning." (*Unfolding Meaning*)

In the struggle to find personal meaning, the question becomes what is the being that endures, the lasting or essential self, the *force of character* as the Jungian analyst James Hillman has called it. For some this search may be a gentle process of settling into that which lies below, as one's authentic self or true nature. As Rabbi Schacter writes in *Aging to Saging,* "Aging is a kind of natural monastery in which earlier roles, attachments, and pleasures are naturally stripped away for us. . . towards 'being.'"

For others the search for meaning may be a more tumultuous process of breaking down and letting go. Florida Scott-Maxwell writes, "Our accustomed shell cracks here, cracks there, and that tiresomely rigid person we supposed to be ourselves stretches, expands and with all inhibitions gone we realize that age is not failure, not disgrace . . . What of that part of us, that nameless, boundless part who experienced the route, the witness who saw so much go, who remains undaunted and knows with clear conviction that there is more to us than age."

Self-knowing gives meaning! "For He who finds his way to the core of the self, whence arises all levels of the I, all spheres of the world, he who finds his way home to his first source with the question, 'whence am I?' is born and reborn." (Maharishi, cited in Metzner, R., *Opening to Inner Light.*)

The Strawberry

The following story is about Margaret, a courageous and self-revealing writer who first began her quest for meaning in elderescence by asking the question, "what is my authentic self, my true nature?"

Margaret was in her eighties when her husband suffered a stroke-related illness and she first began her quest. She found herself searching for tranquility, strength, and self-acceptance as she faced her fear after her husband's death. Margaret is a writer of five novels. When she was eighty-nine, she published her own personal story, part memoir and part investigative reporting, which drew her into the world of nonfiction.

For Margaret, writing has always been an avenue of self-expression. "Writing is a tool to find out what you don't know you know. You are equipped with pen and paper . . . then you begin to know, begin to question it in a way you didn't without the pen. . . . then it begins to come out and one thing leads to another and . . . it is just so amazing . . . amazing, how everybody has a storage of self-knowledge."

She shares her journey toward self-understanding and her search for personal meaning in *Growing up in Old Age*. Written during a seven-year period, it is a compelling, honest, and soul-searching revelation of how she came to accept her authentic self. "In order to face being old with reasonableness and courage I needed to disempower my fears . . . Fears of growing old have finally and forcibly brought to my attention how perishable my counterfeit female superiority and dependencies have been . . . and how obstructionist . . . and still are to the pursuit of a reassuring answer to that question: If there is an inner woman other than the woman I see in the mirror, who is that woman? Are we our names, where we were born, our ancestors, where we live, our friends, our occupations, our appearance, our feelings, our family? After all these are examined it becomes clear that these aspects of our selves are illusive; they can be so easily lost. What within us endures?" She answers, "My integrity, my heart, my love of nature, my values, my innermost being." These are the things that give Margaret personal meaning.

As we drive up the dirt incline and then descend toward the ocean, we see Margaret's house. The scene is breathtaking: a view of rolling hills, the luminescent sea beyond, fronted by gentle pond reeds. Margaret's personal journey, however, evolved in a tent in a field beside her house. One of the last passages from her book describes a moment of insight as she gazed out her kitchen window. "I was invaded by something unidentifiable. Immense. It had slipped in without any forewarning that I was aware of, and had suffused my consciousness. For a moment that was a second or an eternity, I knew that, sitting there, I saw, grasped, encompassed, lived, in a clarity I had never before experienced, the presence of everything in my life as it was at that moment, including myself in appropriate balance with it . . . I was at once experiencing . . . momentarily, with and in that present moment—myself—existing objectively and thus limitlessly with field, pond, sea, kitchen, my husband, my world."

In answer to the question, "Who am I?" she writes, "I am something I see imagistically, as a small area that lies at my center and ticks away . . . a central, isolated, unquenchable entity that lies underneath everything else and that gives origin to it." Margaret believes that this sense of integrity is present all along within oneself; it just needs to be uncovered, remembered.

Looking back to a photograph of herself at age two, she can already see her lifelong struggle with integrity versus fear. That little Margaret already had experienced a war between her own desires and impulses, between her own authenticity and other people's expectations of her. She writes, "She is all apart inside, not all together, afraid all the time . . . composed of warring forces . . . her own do's and other people's don'ts."

Today, Margaret describes a realization of her own mortality which makes her search ever more urgent. "Time is running out . . . I am a woman growing very old and I am afraid of being afraid."

Margaret is not religious, but is a sensitive, spiritual person who has found it is important to live in the present, not in anticipation of what is going to happen next because it will not happen that way anyway. In fact, Margaret's primary antidote to fear is the knowledge that living her life in fear is losing it. "There is not always tomorrow . . . but there is clearly and limitlessly, today."

Though she says she is still searching and always will search, she has found her meaning and purpose for life in "living in the present without judgment (but with) attentiveness and mindfulness. I kept telling myself that now is the only sure moment and that the way to be free of fear is to live in that moment"

Attentiveness and being present in the moment are inseparable: "You can't have one without the other." This awareness came as a result of Margaret's acceptance of the fact that she "was old," a realization that helped her change the way she looked at the world.

Margaret illustrates this viewpoint with the Buddhist parable: a man chased by a tiger hangs from a vine over a cliff as two mice gnaw on the vine. The man spots a strawberry. He picks it, eats it, and savors its delicious flavor.

When the "strawberry" is there in front of you, taste it!

"There is no conscious or purposeful way," says Margaret, " to produce a moment of insight, nor any way at all consciously to make it stay. What it does, it does quickly. It comes; it goes. But though it flashes out almost as soon as it has flashed in, it leaves a message, which is fed back into the accumulated wisdom of the gestalting gestalt, never to be lost."

Living with no immediate answer to "Who am I now?" may be uncomfortable. For in our culture, emptiness is seen as a deficiency, an absence to be avoided. There is little appreciation for "neutral space" as an important place from which we can gain new perspectives, new ways of seeing. Hanging onto our past identities as anchors can disrupt the transitional process of dis-identification with who one has been. If one can let go, and bravely face the loss of what one has known and who one has been, new meaning for the authentic self can emerge.

The *self* is defined as a person's true nature, an intrinsic, deep, personal uniqueness. This self is ageless, maintaining continuity despite the physical and social changes that come with time. In contrast, *identity* is that which provides self-recognition, the things for which one is known. In elderescence, the struggle becomes one of separation between one's true nature and one's old identity. Reclaiming, recovering, or even discovering the essence of one's nature, perhaps for the first time, becomes a major focus for some elderescents. That deep true nature within us, that which survives not only the changing landscape of our lives, but physical deterioration itself, is the source of personal meaning and may even survive death.

Some elderescents acknowledge profound reorientation in their awareness of their public identity. How one has presented one's self to the world, the identity that one has assumed may be revised in this stage. One such elderescent who asked to remain anonymous, spoke of participating in a research project of a friend who was studying personality types. The personality testing revealed an introvert personality type. This was a new concept for him. He had felt during his career life that he had been an extrovert, a compulsive, hard working administrative type, forced to deal and live in the public eye. This revelation was ultimately relieving as he stepped back to review this analysis. He could appreciate how hard he had pushed himself to orchestrate and lead in his work life. He could acknowledge with joy and relief that his authentic self now was more solitary and introspective.

In contrast, another elderescent speaks of 'owning' with joy some extrovert traits. She sees herself as having been inhibited by an intense early message 'Be Proper, Act Proper.' This stymied her more spontaneous nature. Being 'proper' was so essential growing up and led her to constantly question her presentation to the world. She acknowledges now that she loves to talk about herself, has a tendency to monopolize and dramatize in conversations with others. She feels relieved from the burden of a 'proper presentation.'

Jung describes the young person's journey as primarily one of identifying himself as separate from his family of origin, and establishing himself in the world. In contrast, he describes the journey of mid and late life as one of expressing one's uniqueness as an individual. People often have difficulties later in life because they have been false to themselves; they have strayed from their true natures.

Elderescence can offer a period when one has time and space to review one's past and dispel false identities. This brings a sense of continuity to life as one connects with the essential self one has always been. This process may bring forward parts of our selves that have been forgotten, discarded, or even unacknowledged. As Gutmann suggests in *Reclaimed Powers in Later Life*, one can revive the hidden treasures within one's self.

As long as there has been human life there has been both a continuous construction of meaning and debate about the nature of what makes life meaningful. Scholars, psychologists, religious and spiritual leaders are all considering the possibility that in elderescence personal meaning may change radically. Jung was perhaps the first in the fields of psychodynamics and psychoanalytic thinking to study what he called the "second half of life." He proposed that increased self-realization was the task of the second half of life, that it would give unique meaning to one's existence, and that an aging person has a "duty and necessity to devote serious attention to himself." He actually claimed that he preferred to work with people in their elder years, because their childhood complexes would have less hold on them, and they also would be less invested in maintaining an image. However, it is understood that he rarely treated a person in the elderescent population.

Psychoanalysts offer a unique perspective on the journey toward self-knowledge, a journey that includes unearthing messages from the unconscious as well as the conscious mind. While consciousness holds the content of meaning, the language of the unconscious includes dream symbols and archetypal images. Jung offered a guide as to how this process of self-study could unfold.

"We surrender less authentic appraisals of ourselves, we begin to draw together from our personal depths, unfilled longings and untapped reservoirs of being, appropriate to this unique self . . . This process involves reminiscence in a spiraling or circular way that recognizes the unrealized desires of our soul . . . such re-identification in elderhood elicits a creative, continuous process of becoming other than what we were, but at the same time, becoming more authentically what we are meant to be."

Honest review and sincere reflection can provide the elderescent with additional opportunities to revisit psychological problems not resolved in adolescence, issues that were never fully understood or integrated.

One elderescent, so deeply into this journey of self-understanding and the search for meaning, speaks about revisiting an essential trauma point in her life, the death of her father when she was twelve.

"I was never helped to mourn, but rather refused to talk about his death because that would bring on floods of tears from my mother which was very frightening . . . it looked so painful. I remember praying to God to reverse that night."

Only recently, in her seventies, has she been able to face this earlier trauma, and cry and rage at God, whom during her late teens she had discarded as uncaring and then as not even a reality. "I accept the connection between giving up my family's religious faith and the death of my father. I accept that mourning has always been unacceptable, and uncomfortable for me."

Her 'block' against grief kept her from achieving a larger sense of meaning, but her new insights have given her the courage to offer love and tenderness to those who face losses, even to cry along with them. This awareness is important as she reaches for greater self-integrity and looks to a spiritual connection in her life.

With aging we hope maturity comes, illuminating this interest in facing our true Self. Psychotherapy for the elderescent, once a rejected idea by Freud, is being accepted by some therapists today. They view it as a viable experience for those who are depressed, cynical, hypercritical, bored or inexplicably anxious, or for those who want to increase self-understanding and/or heal the emotional scars left over from adolescence.

When prestige is not on the line, some elderescents may feel they have nothing to lose, and will enter the therapeutic process with some anticipation and energy. A major issue in treatment will be whether or not they are going to be viewed as still in the adult stage of life or in elderescence. Will there be an understanding that their values and needs are different from those patients still in adulthood? Will they be helped to realize that a personal meaning is critical? And, will they be encouraged to take an inner journey of self-discovery, regardless of age?

Jung identified seven tasks of aging that offer a fascinating conceptualization of a comprehensive approach toward achieving meaning. Beginning in the fifties or sixties of one's life, the first task is to confront and accept the reality of death. Reviewing one's life follows, logically, as the second task; reminiscing lets one witness one's own journey. The third task addresses the acceptance of life as, indeed, finite. Such a realization may come with struggle, for there will be resistance to letting go of dreams that can never be realized. The fourth task is letting go of the pull of the ego. People in powerful positions, company executives or congressmen and women, often fail at this task, unable to relinquish posts of power until humbled by the onset of senility or fatigue.

Jung's fifth task of aging is the honoring of the Self. In analytic terms the individual performing this task must dig into the unconscious to uncover neglected forces in the psyche, its 'unclaimed powers.' Unresolved issues are confronted and the Self becomes whole; the Self in Jungian terms is the God within. We then see ourselves as part of the great cosmos.

The sixth task allows us to know our reason for being, the meaning for one's life. This ultimate meaning comes from the merging of primordial images from the unconscious with conscious thinking.

The seventh and final task makes possible life as a creative process. The individual owns again the archetype of the child as the creative artist or the child at play. This is the symbol of a rebirth. Life once again becomes playful and possibilities become expansive. Living becomes its own object; the exploration of everything becomes the joy.

A quintessential example of an elderescent who lived out this seventh and final task in the aging process was our American folk artist Grandma Moses.

What reconciles the paradox of life and death, it has been suggested, is creativity. In his last years of life, when Jung was an elderescent, an idea came to him in a dream that launched him upon the most creative endeavor he had ever attempted, an autobiographical work entitled *Memories, Dreams, Reflections* (1963). The project, completed two years prior to his death, suffused the last years of his life with energy, pleasure, and meaning.

Myth

Allan Chinen, author of *In The Ever After* and a psychiatrist practicing in the analytic tradition, speaks to the issue of meaning through the parables of 'elder fairy tales,' analyzing them in the context of the psychodynamic theories of Jung and Erickson. Fairy tales, he believes, can be guides for elders' conscious and unconscious evolution; a process of finding new meaning through religious, social, and psychological transcendence. (*Transcendence* is a term often used in the literature of spirituality and psychology, which usually means going beyond the practical world of egocentric concerns, to rise above, to go beyond human experience to numinous revelations, or, in a religious sense, to ascend to a unity with God.) Chinen uses fairy tales in his work as metaphors for the psychological tasks that the elderescent must complete to reach maturity.

The *Shining Fish,* a European fairy tale that ends his unique little book, focuses on an old couple whose children have all died. Living in poverty on a sea shore at the edge of a forest, they are portrayed as being on the "boundary between land and sea, on one hand, and wilderness and civilization on the other hand." In Jungian symbolism this is the boundary that divides consciousness and unconsciousness. The old man makes a living gathering wood, which means he is "recovering material from the unconscious." One day a stranger gives the old man some gold, which he keeps from his wife by hiding it under the manure pile. His wife, unknowingly, sells the manure the next day. This event is repeated; more gold is given, this time it is hidden in a pile of ashes. Losing the gold forces the old man to confront his greedy and suspicious nature, a process identified by Chinen as a first task in elderescence, self-confrontation and self-reformation. One looks at oneself and in the process of reformation repents for selfish acts.

As the tale continues, the stranger gives the old man a bag of frogs, this time with some advice. "Buy the largest fish you can find." Symbolically the stranger represents the inner Self, or God. The wood gatherer takes the suggestion, transcending his egocentric judgment. He buys the largest fish and hangs it on his rafters. At night, during a terrible storm, his shining fish lights the way for young fishermen to return home.

Metaphorically, through self-transcendence, the old man has brought light to the next generation, but only after he has gone through some psychological development. He has confronted his 'shadow,' repented, and offered to the next generation a bit of practical, problem-solving wisdom.

Reiterating Chinen's analysis of how elders evolve, later life requires that we each must eventually confront our unconscious, i.e., the 'shadow,' the darker, the unacknowledged sides of our personas. The next step is transcending one's egocentric desires, a task requiring introspection and relinquishment. The old man comes out of his journey recognizing and responding to the needs of the younger generations, thus giving 'light' or 'emancipation' to society. He demonstrated trust in his own internal messages, hanging the fish from the rafters, for example. The term for this is *emancipated innocence*, meaning he now can trust his childlike intuition, which is a combination of childlike spontaneity and mature practicality. At the end of this journey, the old man has come to a deep sense of who he is. He has found personal meaning by achieving self-integrity, traversing from self-transcendence to self-affirmation.

Chinen talks further about the challenges of living in later life. Though confronted with many losses, e.g. wealth, health, power, and friends, all of which help to disintegrate the fabric of one's life, the elderescent is still able to move forward by grappling with the unconscious issues left over from childhood.

As Jung also suggested, in the latter part of life one has the emotional strength and maturity to contend with the unfinished business of the psyche. Chinen suggests that in maturing, elderescents turn from their youthful preoccupations with possessions, personal ambitions, societal status, propriety, and popularity, liberating the true self of an elderescent to reclaim its childlike spontaneity.

By "reclaiming wonder and delight in life," freed from the ego needs, (self-transcendence to self-affirmation) the elder can assume the role of *mediator*, stressing communication, and linking the present world with the next, helping the young to achieve a balance between the numinous revelations and the pragmatic needs of society.

In the words of Chinen, "A new dichotomy arises—between individuals who will continue to grow and develop and those who stagnate, between the 'elder' and the 'elderly," between those that are emancipated and those that stagnate.

The evolution of an elderescent's life as illustrated through the motif of the fairy tale, requires no religious, political, or even cultural commitment, just a commitment to enhancing one's later years through discovering new meaning and purpose for the emerging self. The transpersonal spirit (nature) of these tales is non-dogmatic and yet they offer a solid spiritual construct.

The Spoken Word of Religion

Religions have historically been the institutions that offered the form, content, and meaning for what one is to think and be at any stage of life. Meaning, in the Christian and Jewish religious venues, is intricately connected with a belief system requiring faith and acceptance of a theology. Meaning comes from a belief in a divine source, a God. The inner journey toward personal meaning is sought through prayer and meditation, both collective and private. While the elder was to be honored in Biblical times, in many of the Biblical stories their roles seem ambiguous. In native cultures throughout the world tribal ceremonies bestowed status on elders, furnished them with roles, and thus provided them with meaning.

Eastern world religions define the role of elderescents as one of preparation for death. For example, in Buddhism the journey of awakening is described as a process of coping with the later stages of life and as an acceptance of death. Joseph Goldstein, a respected Buddhist scholar, describes the four stages of awakening. First comes the Call to Change; this arises from a feeling that something is missing, bringing a need to question life and everything upon which it is predicated. The next step is the Great Renunciation, during which we question all that we are and all that we have, including our attachments, and begin to let go of our habitual ways of being and doing. The third step is the Great Struggle,—with desire, doubt, fear, and death—a courageous and heroic effort to reach love and wisdom. The Great Awakening is the fourth and final stage. This is when we look back and feel a sense of completion. We acknowledge the laws of cause and effect, understanding that our past actions result in our current experience. We understand life as suffering, the cause of which is attachment and cravings. These steps afford an awakening to freedom and an acceptance of our impermanence.

There are interesting parallels between the stages of awakening described by Goldstein and the experiences of elderescents as they move through the transitions of this life stage. The 'call to change' may be, for some, the call to retire, or simply a call to change other aspects of one's life. Then one begins to question all that one has previously been or had. Often this catapults one into an experience of doubt, fear, and anger. In the process we may look back over our past lives with new perspective, moving into a new understanding of the meaning in our lives. An awakening may occur as we come to accept this as our one and only life, our essential nature as impermanent, and death as inevitable.

William James offers, "Religion in its broadest terms consists of the belief that there is an unseen order and that our supreme good lies in harmoniously adjusting ourselves thereto." Tillich speaks of the central theme in religion as "ultimate concern," and Erickson suggests that in adolescence developing a personal ideology is critical. This involves questioning the family's religious beliefs, as well as society's beliefs, and developing beliefs consistent with the adolescent's own feelings. This crisis occurs again in elderescence when "ultimate concern" is central, "a sense or premonition of immortality . . . as creatively given in the form of world religions."

Undoubtedly, most important for religious people is the belief and experience of a connection to an Almighty God, the creator of all. This belief often bestows on believers the absolute meaning for their lives and a firm sense of direction—one often hears a religious person invoking God as someone who is looking over *them*. It also influences how they relate to the world.

The scriptures of various religions usually provide rules or guidance for how one is to live one's life. Some religions offer a comprehensive design and direction for life, with an afterlife often the ultimate promise. The church, synagogue, or mosque may even become a second home for its members and followers. Most important, belief in a particular religion can provide personal meaning, both meaning that comes from fellowship with others and meaning gleaned from the scriptures and the beliefs themselves. For elderescents committed to a religious affiliation, religion has provided *answers* to questions about the meaning of life and life eternal. They may worry about suffering a physical death but death itself is not something to be feared.

The role of religion in our society today is hotly debated. At the forefront of this debate is whether meaning is embedded in religion or in the human sciences. In the mid-twentieth century psychology became the religion for many, extending to them hope in the belief that meaning would come through self-understanding. Today, spirituality, loosely defined, has captured the hearts and souls of many in this country, as is evident from our interviews with elderescents. A seventy-two-year-old woman defined her spirituality, "as now coming from being in the out-of-doors." Paul Pruyser, who studied both psychology and religion, wrote in 1987 that there is a bipolar phenomenon in religiousness in the aged. Some will become more religious and others will become less involved.

In the process of self-review and reminiscing, elderescents may discover that they have been false to their true natures as a result of religious affiliation. They had made compromises and commitments that served the church or synagogue, etc., but which were not really in keeping with their true selves. The journeys toward self-integrity of religious elderescents can be as intense and difficult as for those without a religious affiliation. The relinquishment of religious roles and affiliations, as well as theological beliefs, may create personal and spiritual havoc, even trauma, as some elderescents reject dogma and search their souls alone.

Some ex-priests tell of confronting their spiritual challenges after Vatican-II, how they found help in a personal therapy journey. Though Jung was not religious, he was indeed spiritual and championed the important role of elderescents as members of society who could best address the ultimate meaning of life. He believed that the meaning of life was to be found in expanding consciousness about the universe. Man would be partner with God. Man would help God know Himself, through man's reflection. Our unconscious would connect us to God. We would be *One*.

The Here and Now

Is a belief in life after death essential for personal meaning and self-integrity in this stage of life? Many of the elderescents interviewed denied a religious affiliation and a need for a sense of an afterlife.

When You Die You Are Dead and That Is It

Stan, a very thoughtful seventy-five-year-old elderescent teacher, writer, and psychologist, says, "When you die you are dead and that is it . . . I am fearful and then accepting. I do not believe in a hereafter . . . When we die, we die . . . that's resolved. It is the dying process that is of concern." This elderescent finds meaning, however, in "spiritual growth which has a focus on seeing life as a process, treasuring the moments one is alive, a beautiful day, '3-D days', low humidity, clear sky, cloudless, and green trees . . . I honor these things . . . having exquisite relationships and wonderful dilemmas. Life is a process of being involved in the moment."

Stan is wary of living either in the past or the future, and seems to be grounded in continuity. "It is central," he declares, and thus his family and his family history are what sustain him. He shared his thoughts about his grandfather, a wise man who told him when Stan was ten that "confusion was the source of wisdom." For Stan, dilemmas are fascinating as a mode of keeping life as a process. He outlined several tasks that give him a very present focus: training and experience in which study and service to others are honored; maintaining loving relationships. He has worked on his second marriage and "now it is delicious." He keeps in contact with his three children. Other tasks are: self-care, seeing the body as a temple and maintaining an active Spiritual Connection. Though he comes from an orthodox Jewish family background, Stan is a Unitarian, which means "understanding increasing dimensions of myself, others and the world."

Stan labeled another task as "male crisis," referring to the challenges of physical decline, both in strength and in sexuality". . . not terribly upsetting though . . . for there is something left—Dialectic thinking, accepting the natural process . . . a patience . . . I don't personalize." He acknowledged that he has been through many personal struggles and these struggles required commitment to resolutions!

The last task on Stan's list is acceptance of mortality in which there is no afterlife.

Stan has authored a book on addiction, which is in the process of being published, and he has a half-time psychotherapy practice. He relates a joy and aliveness in the process of, as he calls it, "life and life as the here and now." This elderescent rejects the idea of a Divine Entity. He believes, however, in a kind of evolutionary force that encourages an inner, personal drive toward an evolving higher consciousness. Accessing knowledge gives meaning to Stan's life.

She Has a Story

She likes to be called Rosie, when you get to know her. Rose Treat is a ninety-five year old "national treasure," artist we interviewed. She is decidedly grounded in the "here and now." Rosie's story is about finding meaning through creativity and a practical sense of living in the present moment.

While in her fifties, Rose found an all abiding passion and meaning for her life, which had emerged out of a health crisis. While recuperating from a year-long illness, Rose and her husband Larry moved to a new home on Martha's Vineyard. Each day, while Larry wrote mysteries, she got up early, walked on the beach, and swam nude in the ocean. She also saw seaweed for the first time in her life, fell in love with this vine of the sea, took it back home, and discovered that she was able to mount it on a mat board.

Rose has actually created a new art medium in her seaweed creations and it has remained her passion, meaning, and purpose for almost forty years. Her works of art have been exhibited in a variety of locations, including Harvard, the Smithsonian, The National Museum of Women in the Arts in Washington, DC, and most recently at the Maritime Museum in Australia. She has taught classes on seaweed art in her home on the Vineyard, as well as on Cape Cod. She has told her story in magazines and on TV and radio.

Rosie's sense of herself, her courage, her tenacity, wisdom, and understanding of life, comes through in the stories she tells. She believes we all have stories, though we may not know it, or know how to tell them, and that stories are the form of expression which best reveal our lives. Her life stories reveal an authentic self and a love of adventure; she knows what attracts her and pursues her instincts. She remembers when, during World War-II, for example, she and Larry lived in a two-hundred-year-old house with bare floors. Rugs were expensive to buy at that time, but she saw an article in the *New York Times* about a rug maker. Rosie called the rug maker to see if she would teach her how to hook rugs. The rug maker agreed and Rosie began hooking rugs, making several for her home and for others. Today, she has a beautiful rug with a scene of a squirrel, trees and flowers hanging in her home.

Rosie has developed self-discipline and is happy to share guidance with others. She offers, "One must take opportunities when they appear. Even if one fails, the trying is a success in itself." She credits her husband, Larry, who was a famous mystery writer, with always giving her courage. Her advice on the choice of a spouse is: "be in love with one's potential spouse's career, since you will be living with it for life."

Rose says she finally married at thirty-four after turning down proposals from lawyers and doctors; she always wanted to marry a writer. She and her husband were married for fifty-five years until his death. Her advice for long life is: "a good marriage and work!" Her wisdom is practical and at the same time profound.

Rose tells another story as we play scrabble in her living room overlooking Sengekontacket Pond. She remembers a neighbor arriving at her door with two big baskets of mushrooms as a gift. Rosie cooked them—they were delicious. Always ready to try new things, she went back to the neighbor and asked him to show her where to find mushrooms growing in the woods nearby. As Rosie's interest in mushrooms increased, she joined the New York Mycological Association, making many wonderful friends with fellow mushroomers. She later joined the Boston Mycological Association and invited both groups to go mushrooming in the State Forest near her home on Martha's Vineyard.

Wonderful weekends followed, with hunting, cooking, drying, canning, and marinating mushrooms. She began to lead workshops on mushroom gathering and became the Island expert on identifying mushrooms. Until recently, she even served as an expert in the local hospital's emergency room, on-call to answer questions about possible mushroom poisonings. People still bring her mushrooms to identify.

One year Rosie, well into her seventies, decided to display some of her seaweed art at the All Island Show at the Tabernacle in Oak Bluffs. When she called the organizer, she was told that they didn't accept that type of art into the show. The next year Rosie didn't bother to call; she just showed up and signed in—and won a blue ribbon! She still has one of those delicate, lovely pieces hanging in her living room.

A visitor to Rosie's studio can see seaweed in each stage of the artistic process, along with a large number of ribbons she has collected throughout the years. Rosie continues to walk the beaches searching for all types of seaweed, though only working for an hour at a time now, since she tires more quickly. She still offers demonstrations in her laboratory to classes of school children.

Rosie, a true example of the creative force coming into its own at mid life, defines her life over the past forty years by her adventures and creative endeavors. One might call it self-transcendence—a woman in her seventies, eighties and nineties nationally honored for a new art form. Now ninety-five with a centeredness that is compelling and a great sense of purpose, she will undoubtedly work at her art until she dies. Whether playing Scrabble or collecting seaweed, she assuredly knows her intent, and how to achieve her goals. Her grounding is in the 'here and now.'

A purpose for being arose when a uniquely individual meaning awakened Rosie's passion, her soul. She discovered something that gave her great personal meaning, working with seaweed, honoring its beauty. She denies any acceptance of the spiritual and certainly is not religious; she may refer to the power of meaning in nature. "The secret in the search for meaning is to find your passion and pursue it."

Rose honors the idea that great freedom comes when one let's life develop in its own way. Her life is an inspiration, and she is loved and admired by the Island community.

Culture and Society

Societies can impart meaning to their citizens. Through its rewards, valued educational, political, social, and even religious meanings are promoted. These can be a source of influence in the development of a personal meaning. In *Unfolding Meaning*, David Bohm said, "We are the totality of our meaning and most of our meaning comes from society." Jung said, "Could by chance culture be the meaning and purpose of the second half of life?" David Gutmann claims that the elder is the conveyor of culture and culture gives meaning for living. In his book *Reclaimed Powers—Men and Women in Later Life* he traces the role of the elderescent in our culture, as well as in many of the native cultures of the world. In traditional societies, such as the Native American Navajo tribe, the Highland Mayas, the Lowland Mayas, and the Druze of Galilee, where folk cultures have endured for many centuries, meaning is imparted to the community via the extended family, through a patriarchy where the elderescent male becomes the guardian of the laws and myths of the tribe.

Gutmann, a renowned psychologist in the study of geronotology since the 1950s began his work "Not to assuage some private guilt about persecuted elders but to build a career and satisfy my curiosity about a large sector of the life cycle, an empty space on the map of developmental and dynamic psychology." In the Preface to the second edition of his remarkable book *Reclaimed Powers* he stresses the freedom that this time of life has allowed him. "Speaking for myself, I am willing (if not actually glad) to join the fight. Elderhood not only brings loss, it also brings liberation. And I have reached the point where I no longer have to worry about building a career, I am freed up to speak truth to power, and to bring the psychotectonic perspective to bear on hitherto unexplored psychological phenomenon—normal and abnormal—of later life." His perspective honors a secular, cultural view of life.

Gutmann asks and answers this perplexing question: "Do the aged exist among us as a side effect . . . or do they represent a vital subplot in the larger human story?" He substantiates with a definite "Yes! Elders are necessary to the well-being of all age groups . . . They fill unique roles, vital to the continuity of their extended families and larger communities, across the range of human societies." Gutmann's effort is to make "more manifest a particular evolutionary design of our species and the developmental character of aging." He then answers the question of whether longevity is a gift of nature or medical technology: "We do not have elders because we have a human gift and modern capacity for keeping the weak alive; instead, we are human because we have elders!"

In conducting extensive fieldwork at the Kansas City Studies of Adult Life, as chief of psychology at Northwestern Medical School, and as originator of the "Older Adult Program" there in 1973, Gutmann has been a hands-on trained observer of developmental changes in aging. He has used projective techniques (T.A.T. analysis), observation as well as interviews, to note definite changes in elderescent males throughout the world as they move from an active to a passive stance. The older these elderescent males were, the more rapidly he saw them "traverse the mastery track toward the passive."

Gutmann describes the elderescent male, observed across a broad cultural spectrum, as becoming more nurturing, sensitive, and passive. In native traditional societies, as in ours, they disengage from their work lives. However, in traditional societies they still maintain meaningful roles within their cultures by assuming other responsibilities and becoming the "culture-tenders." Elderescent males in these cases honor the life transitions, maintain the rituals and the rites of passage, and the cultural heritage of their societies. As conveyors of the values, customs, and struggles of their klans, elderescent males preserve and relate the tribal history, thereby imparting meaning to their lives because of the importance of their roles.

Where male gerontocracy (meaning government by a council of elders) is still in place, the elderescent male's position of respect increases with age. Elder males guard and hand down the folklore, maintaining the religious ceremonies and institutions as well as the "rites de passage" believed to be "linked to the gods." Their domain is culture's sacred powers, ensuring their positions in the community, and giving them personal meaning.

Gutmann suggests that the passive stance of older men may indeed be required for these sacred duties; as conduits to special spiritual power, it's believed the gods may prefer to deal with their humility and passivity. "To repeat, older men may lose the qualities of the warrior, but as these phase out they reveal an understructure of hitherto hidden cognitive and affectional potentials."

Rather than being victims in folk-traditional societies, the aged, particularly older men, are the authentic heroes. "Their special stature has to do with their privileged access to supernatural power sources," says Gutmann, "that they, in effect, create and make real for the rest of the society . . . and in their kin-and culture-tending roles older women ease the parenting trials of young mothers, while older men, by imbuing conforming behavior with mythic, heroic meaning, make domesticity palatable for young fathers."

"Culture is the unique meaning of an otherwise ordinary society," says Gutmann, emphasizing that it is culture that binds a community, attaching people to one another and changing antisocial egotism into a responsible force for the good of the society. In traditional folk societies the elderescent male is deemed a sacred leader, giving power and credibility to the secular rules of the community. He identifies with the gods and reassures his people about death's inevitability, ensuring a safe passage. As these customs and rules, which have evolved from the very beginnings of folk culture, continue to be honored and passed down from one generation to the next, all life in that culture has meaning. The urge, or the freedom, to search for one's own voice and develop an individually tailored sense of personal meaning may never emerge in these traditional folk societies as they do in our culture. If and when the outside world impacts a folk culture, then the struggle to find personal meaning may emerge.

Our culture does not honor or identify any particular segment of the population as conveyors of rituals, rites of passage, or our *tribal history* of values and customs. In contrast to folk cultures, elderescent males in our culture have no identified, or honored role. Gutmann believes that our Western society is in a period of crisis, a "disheartening contrast with folk-traditional assemblage." He believes that in the abolishment of the culture tender roles, we have lost meaning.

His attack on "the victimization" of elderescents as they have experienced it in our society during the past century is convincing: "Ethnographic vignettes from around the planet give clear evidence of the erosive effects, particularly on elder male leadership, of rapid modernization, industrialization and urbanization." He sees elderescents who still hold positions of commercial or political power as simply "older versions of successful young men," perhaps attempting to deny their finiteness. For without an acceptance of death, Gutmann says, elderescence becomes replete with anxiety and defensiveness, devoid of meaning and value. The elderescent in our society, who has truly outgrown the adult stage, will acknowledge that his position of power in the future looks "bleak."

The urbanization of our society throughout the twentieth century has eroded extended family contact and support. Gutmann speaks pleadingly about the plight of unsupported nuclear parents who are unable to "usher the child successfully through the long period of helplessness," unable to give the child a sense of self-respect, meaning, and purpose. Often it is the elderescent who verbalizes this erosion of meaning, values, and lack of family structure in our present society.

In our interview with Walter Cronkite, he expressed the concern and despair he feels about the younger generation. "I do worry a great deal about the younger generation. I might say a cultural value or a quick definition is the collapse of our standards. That bothers me a great deal. Language has taken such a terrible tumble in recent years. The concept of civilized behavior and the concept of civility in our national dialogue seem diminished and these things concern me a great deal. One cannot help but believe that the lowering of our standards and expectations is dangerous to our concept of civilization. And those who organize to make improvements and effect change, unfortunately, seem to have a hidden political agenda. There isn't a concerted effort to do something about it purely for the purpose of improving our standards in education and standards of behavior. The hidden political agenda destroys the worthiness of the cause and the opportunity to organize profitably."

Gutmann's concern for the survival of future generations stresses the need for establishing life-sustaining institutional frameworks that impart cultural meaning to younger generations. Now an elderescent himself, Gutmann makes an impassioned analysis of the critical value of the role of parenting across all generations, and the need for a re-vival of the extended family with elders as *"Emeritus Parents."* Though he decries our culture for having lost meaning, he believes it can be restored by honoring the extraordinary wisdom of the elderes-cent. This wisdom is borne of relinquishing the pursuits of the young adult, letting go of ego-driven activities, and making time for reflec-tion and review, which can provide invaluable guidance.

Secularized societies become most vulnerable to anti-social or crim-inal behavior as the cultural mores are dismissed. Secularism and ur-ban anarchy "becomes the common tragedy." As the traditional posi-tion of elderescents in the community is sacrificed, all the vulnerable segments of society, children and the disabled, for example, become victims. Gutmann's thesis is that "the true 'weak face' of aging is the result of de-culturation, which is associated with urbanization and modernization. Urban de-culturation leads to the loss of community, and values become a private and subjective matter where 'narcissistic preference' dictates the lines of affiliation."

From Stanley Witkin, editor of *Social Work,* "Finding meaning in later life is not an individual act, but the collective understanding of a society whose citizens see beyond their individual desires. Construct-ing a collective, inclusive dignity affirming meaning for the later part of life will come when the voices of older people speaking for them-selves, are salient."

Creativity

Many elderescents offer creativity as a central source of personal meaning. As David Bohm, the notable physicist, writes *in Unfolding Meaning*, "Creativity is an absolute necessity." It is a necessity because creative thinking is what causes new meanings to emerge. The in-scrutable H. L. Mencken offers "If he got no reward whatever, the artist would go on working just the same; his actual reward, in fact, is often so little that he almost starves. But suppose a garment worker got nothing for his labor; would he go on working just the same? Can one imagine his submitting voluntarily to hardship and sore want that he might express his soul in 200 more pairs of ladies' pants?"

Twenty percent of elderescents never retire! They have an inner creative passion that gives them abiding meaning, providing a purpose throughout their lives. Their stories and thoughts give voice to the forces that sustain their commitment to creative work. Many confess that they do not choose to create. It is not a choice! Yet often, despite debilitating illness, they continue to work. Henri Matisse painted some of his finest art in the last years of his life, often confined to a wheel chair or bed. Though his time was waning, Renoir strapped a brush to his crippled hand in order to paint. A female therapist/ colleague, in her late eighties, continues to see patients, and, though she often falls asleep for a few moments during sessions, patients continue to find her help invaluable. To this aged therapist, each new patient is a unique challenge, providing meaning that takes her on a new journey.

The key to continued passion in one's work is a creativity that sustains one through the hard times, whether it is working through a major transaction in the corporate world or writing a great novel. The need and the drive to express what one thinks and feels in and of itself has meaning. This inner capacity to grow sustains the artist in the desire to express his or her sense of self through their productions.

At the age of ninety-five, Al Hirschfeld, an artist noted for his incisive drawings, particularly of actors and actresses, says, "I don't consider that I work, you know. It's something I like to do. The fact that they pay for it and reproduce it, that's gravy!" He calls his cartoon-like drawings "capturing the character of the person." His process of creating is stated in clear, concrete terms. "You take a blank piece of paper and create a problem that didn't exist before and then you solve it to your best satisfaction . . . I'll look at a piece, savoring the thought, and say to myself, 'Did I do that?'" Each piece, apparently, comes in a flash of inspiration.

Hirschfeld worked a full day, seven days a week, but never at night. He attended theater in New York City three times a week, where he could mingle with and observe the people he loved, who were also his inspiration to create.

Riane Eisler, age sixty-six, was by profession a writer and best known for *The Chalice and the Blade*. She loved both life and her work. "I feel that I'm not even one-half the way up the hill and I'm going to keep climbing strong."

And Rose Styron, another elderescent writer speaks of "still escaping, still looking to the next horizon to fly there, still traversing or inhabiting lands only imagined, beyond." Exploring new horizons provides meaning that keeps her climbing. Echoing those words, Liz Smith, now in her mid-seventies, loves her work as gossip columnist and says she knows she'll never stop finding meaning in her writing.

Another elderescent, a choreographer and teacher now in her late-seventies, faced her mortality in 1972 when she was diagnosed with colon cancer. She continued to dance, using her art form to express her inner urge to create, and offering dance as a way to bring about healing. She then offered workshops that celebrate the aging process through dance.

Confirming the fact that artists don't retire, Ruth Asawa, a Japanese artist now in her seventies, says, "Probably artists do live longer because they are doing what they want to do. Time is our own," she asserts.

Artists, writers, and performers do not, however, have a corner on being able to do what they want in elderescence. Activists, entrepreneurs, and indeed anyone who gives expression to their intrinsic selves through creative endeavors that bring meaning to their lives will naturally want to continue their work. These individuals speak of keeping their views of the world and of life open, creating and recreating an inner meaning through their personal avenues of expression.

Matilda Cuomo, wife of the former governor of New York, Mario Cuomo, and a creative activist and mentor at the age of sixty-six, said, "I am so active and excited about what I am doing that I've almost become ageless." And, when Sister June Canoles, member of the Sisters of Notre Dame, and a businesswoman, teacher, administrator, and graphoanalyst, heard that some Sisters were retiring, she said with firmness and conviction, "I'll never retire, I'll drop dead first." She has continued to help create a growing religious community for social justice.

The list goes on. Jane Goodall, at sixty-five, was still having an impact on the natural environment as she solicits money for endangered species. She followed her passion, making the world daily aware of the need for the preservation of the wild and endangered species of Africa.

She had no intentions of stopping her crusade, which is central to her personal meaning.

The founder of the Women's Spirituality Program at the California Institute for Integral Studies, Elinor Gadon, in her seventies, taught at Mills College. "I am passionately engaged in the work I do," she states. "I feel I am at the height of my creativity and intellectual powers."

At her recent memorial service, the remarkable Katharine Graham was proclaimed the most influential woman in America. In her interview with us three years prior, she emphasized that when she stepped down from the directorship of the *Washington Post* and turned the reins over to her son, she was not retiring. In her own words she said, "To me, working is a form of sustenance, like food or water, and nearly as essential."

She spoke about the need to achieve a new creative balance in her life. While retaining her influence at the *Post* as part of a three-person executive committee, she also worked to add new creative initiatives to Washington's educational scene. She gave special attention to community development in Anacostia, a low-income neighborhood in Washington, DC. At the time of her untimely death precipitated by a fall, Graham was attending a conference in Idaho. She found enduring meaning by giving and creating.

Windmills In My Mind

The following interview with an eighty-six year old elderescent demonstrates a rebirth of childlike creativity in elderescence. He unconsciously sees his art as the embodiment of his essence, a meaning he feels a need to express.

At the foot of the hill above the Baltimore Harbor, beside two brick buildings that were formerly whiskey factories, stands a forty-foot-high windmill. Two other large windmills can be found inside the buildings. These fantastic structures, all propelled by wind, are the creations of Vollis Simpson.

The Simpson family farm, a one-hour drive past Raleigh, the capital of North Carolina, is now Vollis Simpson's playground, complete with a pond surrounded by hundreds of wind driven art objects. People come from all over the world to see and purchase Simpson's objects of art, some of which are animals, horses pulling wagons and carts, owls, cats, and birds. Others are people carting water, sawing wood, and airplanes. Each structure has a part that moves in the wind.

Simpson describes his work: "I weld and sand and it's more or less a make-believe. I've got a little tiny pump; the winds turn a little man that also turns. Then there's a little bucket with make-believe water. There is a man sawing wood and right at the end, I have a Christmas tree about a foot high. I've got to send one to California."

Simpson was born and reared on the farmland where he lives today in the house that his father built for his family decades ago. Following in his father's footsteps, as many sons did in his generation, he became a house mover. "I've farmed, I've done house moving; I've done shop work, welding. I've done most everything you can mention," he says. Simpson talks with enthusiasm and pride about the shop he built when he came home from World War-II. "I fixed anything anybody wanted. I worked night and day."

In his mid eighties, Simpson retired from repair work, closing his shop and turning it into his art studio. He traces his love of mechanics back to his time in the Air Corps in 1940, when he was a young draftee. (He had been in the service for one year when war broke out.) Living conditions were primitive on Saipan, where he was stationed for five years during the war in the Pacific. Clothing had to be washed in the ocean, a circumstance that inspired Simpson to begin working on his wind-powered inventions. Gathering different metal parts from wrecked planes, he created a washing machine, which was run by wind power.

His wife Jean says, "It was already there in his head. He is an engineer . . . he's never had any formal training, but he's got something in there that makes everything jibe at the right time. It all balances and moves at the same time. You have to see for yourself to really appreciate it." Meaning came through his creativity, waiting for the right moment to be expressed.

When Simpson stopped working he was able to devote all of his time to art, his true joy. As his wife remembers, "He retired 'cause he thought time was catching up with him. He said he wanted to be able to put more time to his art. At that age he knew we can't always be here forever. He wanted more time to work on that. He does it full time. He's there from early morning until it gets night. He really enjoys it. He loves it Himself."

His personal history is revealed through his art, which is based on the everyday life he knows and loves so well. "Yeah, I've been there. I've got a man playing a drum . . . my son was in the band in high school. It's about twenty feet, playing and tapping his foot. I've got two horses pulling a wagon, all eight legs walking, wagon wheels are turning . . . I make a lot of knick-knacks, ice cream scoops, and any little breeze will turn them. Anything I do works with wind, except a few pieces that run by electric motor, to put inside museums."

What makes this story so compelling is that here is a man, now eighty-six, who truly expresses his passion, giving him personal meaning. One hears this in his voice as well as in his wife's proud descriptions. "He can work twelve hours a day when he has something in his head."

Simpson has turned his hobby into a thriving, joyful, and lucrative business that gives people pleasure all over the world. Not surprisingly, he indicates that he does not plan to retire from his creative work. "As long as my health is good and I am able to go . . . I've been blessed. You have to have something to do, to occupy yourself, to keep busy; the old man can cut you off at any time."

I am Totally Blissed

A retired social worker turned quilter describes her new joy in creativity. "It has been one year since I retired and yet not a day goes by that I don't feel thankful and totally blessed. When I sit down to read or sew, thrill, almost visceral in nature, rises up momentarily, every day, at least once. I knew I would like retirement, though what has surprised me is the almost giddy joy that I still feel! I think that for the last thirty years I have wanted to stay home and for the last seven years I have been planning to become a quilt maker, collected fabric and equipment, and took lessons on the side.

"The days whiz by, the weeks too. I set a loose schedule now, allowing a thirty-minute nap, often working right through lunch, then rush downstairs and grab a bite to eat. I just love staying at home. I belong to three quilting groups and have three special quilting artist friends who critique each other's work. I work with a group from my church, help with the annual Christmas quilt raffle. As I think over this transition I see that I have traded my outside career work for my life at home as a quilter. I am a Quilter now! I work now at my own pace and direction. I am totally blissed."

Many elderescents, retired from high powered, professional jobs shared their journey discovering great joy in untapped artistic 'potential'. They just knew this was a time to find out what they could enjoy doing! Some said they wanted less responsibility and more time in which to express themselves. For some their newly discovered avenues of expression evolved as they experimented with classes in different art forms. "I think it definitely evolved, " or " I didn't have any particular expectations. I just knew that this was the time to do what I enjoy doing." Life had great meaning and passion for them as long as they could continue to share their creations. Optimistically, one man said, "I think we all have creative potential, whether we realize it or not!"

Elderescents driven by passion to create, whether as artists, sculptors, musicians, writers, inventors, activists, or entrepreneurs, do not seem to seek retirement. Perhaps this is because their work provides both flexibility in lifestyle and work time, and a framework for expression of their intrinsic sense of self. They find different ways of expressing their view of the world and their life remains open to new expressions of their personal passions.

The Age Work Wave

Two wise scholars of human behavior, Erich Fromm and Sigmund Freud, each offered the same essential prescription for a meaningful life, 'love and work.' Katharine Graham, former publisher of the *Washington Post,* spoke of what working meant to her. "Working is a form of sustenance like food and water . . . as essential." Many of the elderescents we interviewed pronounced "retire!—never!" or "I don't like the term retirement!" Many others, however, indicated that they had reduced their working hours to part time. Some who had retired from their previous job commitments expressed great joy at returning to some form of work. "I am so happy to be back in the Main Stream. It keeps me involved . . . gives me some structure."

An eighty-seven-year-old elderescent describes how, at the age of four, he began working at "pulling out nails," for his father. This established a strong ethic. He now has a case load of clients, consults at a hospital, is involved in a research project, and plays tennis three times a week. For him life's meaning is about doing, following one's passion. This gives him a sense of mastery and (his word) "sisu," the Finish name for, "When all else fails reach deep down and still prevail."

Our society adheres to a strong work ethic, a cultural message transmitted largely through our families. "What kind of work will you 'do' when you grow up?" is a question often asked; as adults we "show and tell" by example that life's meaning is found in work. *The New York Times,* in its March 21, 1999 issue, reported, "up to a quarter of older men who are out of the labor force would leap back if they could find a suitable job." In a recent survey in AARP's *Modern Maturity,* November 2002, seven out of ten respondents in the forty-five to seventy-four age group reported they intended to keep working throughout their 'retirement years.' This survey indicates a greater desire to continue working, at least part time, than in 1985.

In today's world very few who retire stay retired. Though major health problems can plague many elderescents, medical science often makes it possible for them to resume working. Many explain that being at loose ends (the "betwixt and between") is demoralizing, depressing, and unhealthy, while work continues to provide a personal, central meaning to one's life.

For some elderescents their sense of self appears fragile without opportunities to remain productive and make contributions. Many tell of feeling a '*dis*-ease,' a feeling of being unsettled until they have performed some work activity each day, whether volunteer or paid employment. For these elderescents work has always bestowed deep satisfaction, a strong sense of themselves, and an identity to hang onto. This construct can be a powerful source of energy and indeed, for some, a purpose to sustain their lives.

On January 12, 2003 Morley Safer, a correspondent on the CBS program *Sixty Minutes,* said, "There's something happening in America. It's called the Age Wave, a social revolution that's changing the way we think about work, about retirement, about what to do with the last quarter of our lives . . . Tonight, we take a look at the shape of things to come." What followed was a parade of individuals in their eighties, nineties, and one at the age of one-hundred-and-two, who all spoke of their commitment and joy in working.

A ninety-year-old woman works thirty-seven hours a week as a machinist. Her sense of self clearly comes from her work. "I would be bored to death sitting and doing nothing . . . I'd be all stiffened up." Work clearly sustains her. In her words, she "would die without it."

The owner of a competitive, aggressive Needle Company who employs many people in the later stage of life declared, "People are here for life. As long as they can climb the stairs, be productive, get along with people, I will promise to find them something to do." During the recession of the late 1980s he needed to hire a number of people who could be flexible and work part time. He related how a 'light bulb' went on in his head; he found his workers among a group of older people willing to work part time. To this day, they are a valuable segment of his labor force.

Safer also interviewed an elderescent scientist at the age of 102 who works nine hours a day five days a week. "How can this be work?" asks the scientist. "This is so interesting. Look, I am finding out what's going on." He adds, "I have an inner movement, an inner drive. And this goes on and it is still going, and I don't have sense enough to quit." Another ninety-one-year-old interviewee "was a half century older than the power shovel" he operates in a quarry. With humor he says, "So I reckon I'm just crazy about a shovel. So I'm going to work as long as I can get up and down off of it."

These elderescents' lust for life; meaning is derived from their productive engagement with ideas, colleagues, and the visible results of their efforts to keep 'doing.' Phyllis Moen, a sociology professor at Cornell University, says work is what America is all about. She further suggests that "volunteer service . . . or paid work is the key to successful aging . . . (to) lower symptoms of depression, greater satisfaction with life and retirement, great health and even longevity."

There has indeed been a dramatic shift in our paradigm about what elderescents can do! As we acknowledge the prominence of the work ethic in this country, i.e. the meaning that work has always had in our culture, and reflect back on the message of mandatory retirement, that one is "over the hill," or "obsolescent" when one reaches the age of sixty-five, we can appreciate the psychological devastation experienced by elderescents during the twentieth century. Today, with new understanding, we can see the meaningful gifts that people in their elderescence can give to society.

I Want to Help

"I will never totally retire," offered Lee, a self-identified "workaholic" who was a dedicated successful minister for thirty-seven years in Christian service. When he retired from the ministry he became a full time organic farmer. In the late 1980s, while still a full-time minister, Lee began experimenting with organic farming and selling produce at markets. "I thought of farming as another calling," he explained. Two themes emerged from our interview with Lee: the importance of his religious faith and the importance of work in his life.

As a young boy he struggled with feelings of inadequacy. "In high school I was a very mediocre student, socially awkward, with a fragile self esteem . . . I was a leader with younger boys in Boy Scouts and the 4H, but I did not compete well with my peers except in varsity basketball. My main ego boost came from adults who thought of me as a morally good, hard working adolescent. In college, because it was 1946, two thirds of my entering class were veterans and they were obviously more mature, smarter, and better adjusted, I thought. I no longer had the close support and encouragement of my hometown adult community; and at first, it was overwhelming peer competition. I worked in college 25 hours a week, which helped boost my self-image. A very important part of my college life was attending the college chapel services and the Methodist College Youth group each Sunday. One Sunday, and I remember the date to this day, it was December 9th, I had attended two church worships and two Christian student groups. I was returning across the Arts and Science Quad at 10:00 P.M. after escorting my girlfriend to her dorm when I had an unexpected *vision.* I had a visual picture of Jesus in my mind and he was smiling at me. I was so moved by the experience that I ran the remaining mile to my room, told my roommates and then called my girlfriend. This vivid memory has remained, having a powerful impact on my faltering self esteem." During his senior year in college, Lee said, "I felt called to full time Christian Service."

"Years later while studying to be a minister in seminary, (at Boston University and Yale) I came across one of Paul Tillich's sermons entitled, 'You Are Accepted.' I felt I was given a context in which to understand that experience. I realized that in the smile of Jesus, I was accepted by God. I was accepted not because of anything I had done, but by the grace of God; I was a unique and important human being. I no longer had to compete with peers or please adults to make myself acceptable. My image of Jesus smiling at me was the beginning of the most important relationship of my life. The loving and gracious God whom I had heard about became real and personal. A steady, growing sense of confidence and purpose emerged in me. I began to read the Bible daily, study and pray. Toward the end of my junior year I was nominated to be president of four student organizations. The shy, struggling, awkward adolescent had evolved into someone perceived as a leader. I believe it was the relationship initiated and sustained by God which was responsible for my success, eventually earning a Doctor of Ministry degree at Boston University."

This was an epiphany that changed Lee's life and gave him a direction for his drive to work and help others. It is perhaps from his grandmother that he learned to honor hard work as virtuous. "She was something of a saint." "Hard work never killed anybody," she would tell Lee. "As a young person I remember her rising at five in the morning, scrubbing the kitchen floor, and doing other household chores before going out into the fields."

"It is very challenging to solve problems and meet the needs of others. My self esteem is enhanced by the number of people I can help. In both the ministry and farming there is always something to do. In the ministry it was hard to ignore the needs of the parishioners. I tend to feel guilty if I have the capacity to solve a problem and I do not do it. In farming, though, it is your planning that can exceed reality, not other people's problems."

Today Lee identifies himself as a workaholic, a compulsion which he shared, stating that "I have struggled against it since I identified the negative effect of over-work forty years ago. Being a workaholic is particularly problematic as I age and I can no longer be as productive as my compulsions expect. Society in general places a high value on work and success generated by work. This makes retirement a difficult adjustment for many. But like other addictions, abuse of work can have a devastating effect on mental and physical health." As a full time organic farmer Lee worked ten hours a day and as a minister he had worked eighty hours a week.

His present challenge is to set reasonable limits on his desire to help people. Lee has a new sense of self-reflection as he suggests, "I am intentionally reducing the expectations I place on myself." He speaks of wanting more balance now in his life. "I want to be a good husband and grandfather and helpful to my community. "There is never any end to people in need and the need for justice and compassion is always there. If it were not for my abiding faith that God is at work in these areas of need, I could easily be overwhelmed and discouraged. But I know that I cannot control every outcome. I am finally not the savior that I might like to be. I can be helpful and useful in God's ongoing work of compassion, justice and peace. I trust God to use my efforts and that of others for ends far greater than my modest efforts. I am comforted by words that St. Paul wrote to Timothy, "No act of love is ever wasted." This thought is helpful in achieving a balance in 'retirement'. In my younger days it was hard to distinguish what I should, could, or really wanted to do. I still have the initial impulse to offer my help, but now I can accept that being sympathetic is often all that is needed or all that I can do. This inner acceptance moderates my compulsions to do, and I can let go and say, 'No!' and actually feel good about making that stand."

At this time in his life Lee accepts himself as a loving, caring, and worthwhile human being, allowing himself more freedom to choose from a variety of possibilities. He values his wife as a counterweight to his tendency to over work, and understands his tendency to be a workaholic. Though he says he will never stop working in meaningful ways, he has achieved a balance, and personal contentment along with it.

"I Have Been Tired and Retired"

Jim is another elderescent who says he'll never stop working. Since first retiring at the age of sixty-seven, he has reinvented himself many times over, retiring *four more times* and working at five different jobs.

"Before I went into the Army I dropped out of high school when I was sixteen and went to work in a factory. I had four years of factory experience. I know the reality of what that is like. For the blue collar worker there is often not a lot of meaning in work. This was my experience; it is probably the same for the support staff in offices.

"I am thinking that I feel better when I do something; it helps to structure my time better. I have had to work since I was sixteen years old, so I am not used to structuring my free time. I do not have hobbies and I don't play golf or bridge." When we interviewed Jim he was seventy-nine and teaching small seminars and mentoring a blind student. He finds that when he is between things he becomes bored, and suffers from a mild cabin fever; his sense of meaning and purpose are suddenly gone. His teaching and mentoring relationships remain at the core of his life, providing meaning for his life, and grounding him in his identity. He says, "I figure that is my contribution. I never invented a wheel, patented a zipper, or a light bulb. I have a lot of pleasure and a lot of satisfaction out of teaching and mentoring."

"For the "grunt" worker, on the other hand, work might have little personal meaning beyond making a living. While making a living is an honorable purpose, retirement and a pension may offer relief from a work life that is likely to be tedious and unpleasant. Still, the question remains, as it does for other elderescents: "What do I want to do now?" The essential journey for each elderescent is "what will bring meaning into my life, give me joy and satisfaction?"

Discovering one's passion or what brings meaning into one's life can feel enormously satisfying, even miraculous, at this stage of life. For those who speak of work as their source of meaning, there is always some attribute of their work or a goal that makes their work valuable to others. In any endeavor this goal will impart a feeling of 'mattering' to another or to society as a whole.

In the words of Joseph Campbell, "If you follow your bliss, you put yourself on a kind of track that has been there all the while, waiting for you, and the life that you ought to be living is the one you are living. Wherever you are—if you are following your bliss, you are enjoying that refreshment, that life within you, all the time."

The Transcendent

Self-transcendence is a term used by gerontologists and psychologists, Erickson and Jung, for example, as well as by scholars referring to religious or spiritual development in aging. Self-transcendence embraces maturity and wisdom, a rising above and beyond the limits of the ego. Used in a religious context it can imply surpassing human understanding, a unity with God or the cosmos. Confucius was perhaps the first to suggest the idea that in aging one transcends the self, the egocentric self in particular. He conceptualized six stages of human development, indicating the sixties as a time in which the individual accepts divine dictate. At seventy the individual accepts heaven's bidding, no longer experiencing a split between personal drives and the heavenly calling.

"Life is the Childhood of Our Immortality"

Our interview with Dr Henry presents a beautifully articulated awareness of change in focus and values. Henry is someone who honors the issue of 'ultimate concern.' At seventy-eight his new sense of meaning comes from his psychological and spiritual sense of a wholeness and connectedness to all and to God.

Henry writes brilliantly of his thoughts on meaning in this stage of life, beginning with a quote from Goethe, "Life is the childhood of our immortality . . . This period of life demands as much study and preparation, as do the other phases of life."

Henry identifies retirement as the "last major developmental task of life," the time when he entered a new phase of his life. "In order to meet this life challenge there must be adequate preparation. We must explore this unexplored territory in order to find the many realms by which we can continue to be an asset to this life process."

For Dr. Henry a spiritual foundation is essential. "One's spiritual status must be assessed and organized in order to give this final phase of life a solid foundation. There must be the acceptance of mortality . . . the necessity of building a realistic belief system in the reality of God . . . A belief in some form of afterlife would seem to be an important building block in the pursuance of this final segment of one's life."

Dr. Henry was a Catholic priest until 1977 when he left the priesthood. Subsequently he developed a private psychotherapy practice and began consulting for a clerical and religious service. He married in 1982. He suffered a stroke in 1984 at the age of sixty. He was frightened, he said, but has learned to live with angina. He continued to work full time at several jobs until 1994 when he took five years off to travel with his wife. His wife recently reminded him that it had been a hard time for him, as he was often depressed. Leaving a full-practice and his professional life as a caregiver behind, he felt a profound loss of meaning. "Life is empty without meaning," he noted. "Introspection became a strong focus."

He began reading biographies of great leaders, Alexander the Great, Napoleon, and Roman Catholic popes, etc., looking for guidance. In his reflection and self-review he discovered a need to develop an acceptance of death as the fundamental block of meaning. "All have to face death . . . Until this reality can be accepted comfortably, progress is not possible. This step demanded a spiritual outlook with some form of a positive God and afterlife at its core. Formal ritual becomes an agent and not a goal. With this in place meaning could come about . . . Introspection became circumspection."

Coming to grips with his belief system, accepting God and a hereafter, Henry rejoiced in returning to the mainstream. With deep pleasure he tells about having "gone from medication for hypertension, angina, stroke, and stomach ailments to no medications except one, which stabilizes normal prostate difficulties."

Turning his attention from his inner journey to the external world, Henry found meaning in a strong belief in God, a spiritual connection with life after death, and new purpose. He returned again to chaplainry and to serving in a psychological capacity for his community's police department. "I am on 24/7 call for emergencies, death notification, etc. . . . I feel that meaning is now once more part of my life and at the same time I am able to control my activities with my growing limitations. I am so happy to be back in the main stream."

Henry characterizes many elderescents who speak of their transitional processes as spiritual journeys that are not defined by a particular religious affiliation but still construct a decided meaning for life. It is a spirituality that gives meaning to those who experience a transcendental wholeness within one's self and in the world. Henry's philosophy reflects several of the themes offered by Jung and Erickson, e.g., changes in one's sense of self are confronted as identities are lost and new identities are assumed.

Personal meaning develops out of self-inspection, and self-affirmation occurs when a firm, deep sense of who one is, "one's one and only self" is realized. Confronting the finiteness of life is expressed as essential to this process. For Henry accepting a spiritual dimension to life and a faith in life after death brought peace, new energy, a belief in a wholeness, or oneness of everything, and an ultimate meaning, a self transcendence that there is more beyond our bodies. As Henry was called again to be a contributor, he found meaning in being grounded in the external community. Dr. Henry speaks of a "self-transcendence," a spiritual dimension of living in this stage that has allowed him to truly accept death.

The term *gero-transcendence* originated with Lars Tornstam in 1989 to describe "a shift in meta-perspective, from a materialistic and rational vision to a more cosmic and transcendent meaning to life, normally followed by an increase in life satisfaction . . . The gero-transcendent individual experiences a new feeling of cosmic communion with the spirit of the universe, a redefinition of time, space, life and death, and the redefinition of the self . . . the individual might also experience a decreased interest in material things and a greater need for solitary 'meditation.'"

Initially Lars Tornstam offered this concept as a counter to the 'disengagement' theory popular in the 1970s which emphasized social withdrawal for the elderescent. He notes that in experiencing gero-transcendence, one does not withdraw into loneliness and depression, but rather assumes a meditative and reflective stance, at times comfortable in solitude but not withdrawal, self directed enjoyment but not loneliness.

In 1997 Joan Erickson, revised her husband's book *The Life Cycle Completed* (1998) which he had written in 1964. She added a last chapter, "Gero-transcendence" following in Lars Tornstam's footsteps. Erik Erickson, who had been the noted authority on life stages, had expected that at some point he would add a ninth stage, but never did. In the book's revised version, Joan Erickson identifies gero-transcendence as an "alternative meta-theoretical paradigm." This theory may or may not be seen as a religious development. Joan was ninety-three when the last chapter was added; though apparently not in the stage of gero-transcendence herself, she resonated with the sense of peace it afforded some. She writes, "I am not retired, serene and gracious. In fact I am eager to finish this revision of the final stage before it is too late and too demanding an undertaking."

Joan described gero-transcendence as a process of maturation and wisdom, when the competitive race comes to an end. A 'letting go' can occur but does not necessarily imply a lack of vital involvement. The normal societal model for old age has been to encourage letting go, rather than seeking a new life with new meaning, new roles—a new self. In contrast, gero-transcendence is seen as a spiritual transcendence from the worldly egocentric concerns towards a more numinous experience. This concept honors significant changes in elderescence, changes which are not seen as defensive mechanisms against the reality of aging but as

signs of an increasing transcendence of personality toward greater individuation. Gero-transcendence implies that the elderescent has come to
the farthest stage in the evolution of individuation and that transcendence increases with age.

Wisdom of the Old Tennis Player

The following thoughts from Dr. Bender will help to portray the experience of gero-transcendence. Dr. Bender, who was seventy-three at the
time of our interview, felt a decided shift in his feelings and focus after suffering a major heart attack at the age of sixty-seven. Success and
making money were suddenly less important. He also experienced a
change in attitude toward death; he no longer feared it. He says, "whatever happened in the 'twilight zone', I now see death as positive, not
an absolute ending. Life is now trying to minimize my ego, giving support with an oriented enhancement to my intuitive self."

Though a student in the true sense of the word all his life, he now
describes meaning as originating from his intuitive self. "The body
concerns drop off and there is a continuation of the intuitive self,
meaning there is something after death . . . I feel freer, have a sense of
wisdom, insight, and confidence. In working with my students I find I
seem to say the right thing at the right time, not really knowing how I
know that. I experience a frequent feeling of connecting with people
that I never connected with before . . . Energy-wise, I have more energy, soul energy, spiritual energy. As there is a winding down of the
body, there is also an increase in spiritual life energy, very physical and
I am amazed how well I perform in different situations. It seems like a
facility."

Dr. Bender uses a tennis metaphor to further describe this phenomenon. "When you are an old tennis player you do not run back and
forth as much, but you seem to be right where the ball is to make the
play."

A new inner confidence has allowed Dr. Bender to decide to ride out
several forms of cancer, rather than accept the more traditional mode
of treatment that would include surgery and chemotherapy. He does
not fear death. With guidance from a Chinese healer, he is doing well
after two and a half years living with two cancers. He has confidence
in what he is doing and a sense of self-integrity, a confidence in his intuition, seeing clearly a unification with everything.

Dr. Bender has had three careers, beginning as a priest, leaving the priesthood in his thirties, obtaining a doctorate in theology and later a doctorate in psychology. He now teaches and has a psychotherapy practice. Though he always has been fascinated by philosophy and theology, he says he is now less drawn to 'heady and abstract' thinking. Meaning for him comes from "a self sense, a core internal cohesiveness, an awareness of an interdependence to everything." His thinking is less conflicted and complicated, and his interest in highly formulated abstract ideas has diminished, replaced by "being in the moment."

Dr. Bender's affinity for paradoxes is apparent: "There are a lot of pieces to life's puzzle that do not fit together; no one has all the answers. Paradoxes are much more evident but not at all 'befuddling' and I experience no effort or need to resolve them."

In terms of his spirituality, Dr. Bender says that it has grown from a more traditional religious beginning. "There are sharp boundaries in each religion," he says, "but in my spirituality there are more undefined levels." He indicates that he relates to a higher power without defining it or becoming dogmatic, and has a fascination with mysticism and a connection to the cosmos. He coined a phrase "baptizing thinking" in reference to his focus in teaching his students.

Dr. Bender now has a deep appreciation for solitude, but doesn't ascribe to it the image of loneliness so often assigned to the elder's years. His is a solitude that nourishes, as is often true for many in this stage of life.

In reference to appreciating the need for finding a 'map' for this time of life, making him aware of its purpose, he says, "It has a uniqueness, a positiveness, a specialness that must be articulated."

Finally, Dr. Bender states that he has found meaning in his life's experiences. While he had been questing through the world of intellectual studies and religion, in the end it was his 'twilight zone' experience that became a catalyst for his profound shift in his sense of meaning, causing him to accept a higher power, to ascribe to a belief in an afterlife, and to redefine his contribution to his students, encouraging them to think for themselves.

Lars Tornstam suggests, "We would expect to find many different degrees of gero-transcendence in old people; not everyone will automatically reach a high degree of gero-transcendence with age. Rather, it is a process which, in optimum circumstances, ends with a new cosmic perspective."

Gero-transcendence, in short, can signal a change in one's perception of the self and one's relation to others, which is identified as ego transcendence, i.e., when ego concerns diminish.

In gero-transcendence one looks forward and outward to a new view of one's self and one's world. In Erickson's conceptualization of the stages in aging, the elderescent is described as looking back to the life lived. Transcendence, on the other hand, implies an active, vibrant process. It signals a decrease in superfluous social interactions, decreased interest in material things and self-centeredness, and more time spent in meditation. These aspects of this state are similar to those defined in Chinen's analysis of elders' fairy tales: a transcendence of ego, a cosmic communion, and the letting go of the material. Cosmic transcendence is a change in perception of time, space, life, and death.

Ready to Ascend

One elderescent interviewed over the course of five years clearly speaks to her experience of transcendence. Kathleen, now eighty-two, often uses the term "transcendence" in conversation. She was born into a large Catholic family and bore three children herself. Late in life she received a doctorate in psychology, became a psychotherapist, and moved outside the faith of her family, a shift that is apparent in her conversation and use of expressions. In our first interview she described herself as a "people person." Indeed, Kathleen is always ready to talk and to share her wisdom, and speaks readily about her changing sense of detachment from the battles of life. Though she still had a small private practice at the time we initially spoke, she verbalized the possibility of future changes in the work arena: "I've done it. I don't need to make any big contributions. I don't think of being old. I want to make time to just be . . . to search myself."

Two years ago, after dealing with medical problems which she deems 'challenges,' she gave up the practice she had been "so involved in." She now spends her mornings reading a great variety of articles and books pertaining to psychological and spiritual ideas, and meditating. And yet, she is very definite about "still wanting to make a difference . . . to have an impact," though she speaks now of being aware of the end of life. "I am closer to it, but I am not scared." Perhaps this is because she sees all of life as a "gift" and has a belief in something after death.

Kathleen often ends her verbalized thoughts with an expression of gratitude. One favorite is "everything is for the best," indicating her belief that everything that happens has a meaning. Her evolution is clear as she so often, beautifully and generously, shares an empathic understanding and acceptance of all humanity. A year earlier, she shared with us her struggle with feelings of irritation toward an individual with whom she had occasional contact. Through introspection and reflection, including taking responsibility for her own feelings and issues, she was able to become open and empathic toward this individual. She had a determination and sense of personal responsibility to resolve feelings she did not want to have toward another human being.

Kathleen often says, "We are all One," a phrase that identifies her cosmic transition, and her struggle to remove the boundaries that separate her from others so that understanding and empathy can occur.

When we first interviewed her, Kathleen spoke about needing to let go of her ego. "I am getting there," she says now, also indicating that she has little interest in material things, possessions, and ego-driven ventures. Kathleen clearly seems to have reclaimed the wonder and delight in life itself, and is a most enjoyable and joyous person to be with. Through meditation and self-reflection she has been able to "let go" (a phrase she often uses) of old hurts and anger and to be in, and appreciate, the present moment.

Kathleen is another elderescent who enjoys her solitude, informing us that she does not experience it as loneliness but as a rich time to be with and enjoy herself. While she has always been a "people person," she now describes enjoying developing other sides of herself. "I am a researcher," she recently chuckled, noting her willingness to share information through her recorded tapes and books of interest to her.

Today any block in the road is a challenge to Kathleen, one to be surmounted with patience and reflection. Her beliefs include a oneness of all life, a consciousness of the cosmos, and a faith in a divine source. She has no fear of leaving her human body and often uses the phrase, "when I ascend." Her long journey of self-discovery has revealed deep meaning for her life, an increase in life's satisfaction, no fear of death, and, in a transcendent sense, the fact that life and death are one.

Richard Griffin, a former priest, also speaks clearly of his spiritual life as an elderscent. "I turn daily to the Spirit within me . . . Death, in prospect, seems to me the greatest of all adventures. Eternal life remains the bedrock of my belief about the after-death experience . . . But I do not know the shape it will take . . . I can feel free to do what I wish. I see spiritual maturity as my goal. Instead of decline, the underlying model of the interior life is on an ascent." (*Aging and the Religious Dimension*)

Lars Tornstam and colleagues surveyed 912 individuals ranging in age from seventy-four to one hundred years of age. They were asked to assess qualities of experience or feelings that were embedded in their concepts of gero-transcendence. Tornstam concluded that a high percentage of respondents "recognize in themselves the qualities of gero-transcendence." Examples of responses on questionnaires include the following:

"Today I feel to a higher degree, how unimportant an individual life is, in comparison to the continuing life as such."

"Today I feel a greater mutual connection with the universe, compared to when I was fifty years of age."

"Today material things mean less, compared to when I was fifty."

"Today I have more delight in my inner world, thinking and pondering, compared to when I was fifty."

Most notable in this study was the high positive correlation between cosmic transcendence and the individual's sense of satisfaction with life. Meaning for these elderescents comes through their transcendent experiences, rather than social pursuits, though these social activities do bring joy and satisfaction. Individuals who scored low on the gero-transcendence scale scored low on life satisfaction. Noted were some differences among socio-economic groups and levels of education of the participants. Tornstam's analysis suggests that those with higher cosmic transcendence scores were more likely to have experienced a greater degree of personal freedom, i.e., to "let life develop unrestricted." Crisis in one's life was often an impetus to experiencing a new reality, a new meaning for life. An age-depression scale that was used did not correlate with cosmic transcendence or ego transcendence. There was no suggestion of a correlation between the use of psychotropic drugs, depression, or psychological stress and gero-transcendence.

Western society has assessed the nature of aging variously as a 'giving up' or disengagement from the activities of adulthood, or the exact reverse, as in staying active and engaged. As a society we are just beginning to honor the idea of transcendence as a developmental process of aging. It is a paradigm that posits, "You and I as not separate objects but as parts of the same entirety . . . past, present, and future are not separate but exist simultaneously." This increase in a cosmic awareness relates to feelings of oneness with nature, the ocean, plant life, and the oneness of all living creatures. As one seventy-three-year-old elderescent exclaimed sitting and reflecting at the edge of a pond one day, "I am part of all this nature. I am one with it. I feel it. I know it."

Ego drives become insignificant. The individual experiences himself as part of a cosmic flow of energy. Fear of death is diminished. The quantum physicist David Bohm offers similar thoughts about this shift in consciousness in his book *Unfolding Meaning*. Bohm refers to the unknown or unknowable as the "implicate order," a universal wholeness of enfolding and unfolding of meaning.

We have suggested in this book that meaning can come from culture, personal experiences and backgrounds, and education, all enfolded into a sense of self-integrity. Meaning pervades our being and yet meaning is hard to define. Bohm says that the whole of meaning, as in our thoughts about meaning, will never be fully defined, though it is the essence of our consciousness: "Without meaning there would be no consciousness. Meaning is capable of indefinite extension. If meaning is what life is then a change in meaning is a change of life."

He speaks further of "the need to change the ego so as to end fragmentation . . . by healing the sin sick soul . . . (for there is) the possibility of the extinction of mankind that is implicit in our general fragmentary way of life."

Gutmann talked of the fragmentation of culture and the disastrous effects of deculturation. Jung's thoughts on human oneness in the collective unconscious, the universal archetypes, signify a unity that ends fragmentation. Elderescents on a spiritual path speak of a cosmic transcendence that expresses hope in a universal oneness. Each of these theories projects the transcendence of the ego, letting go of that which has separated us from each other. Susan Eisenhandler in *Aging and the Religious Dimension,* offers, "Understanding the integrated meaning of one's life is the only effective foil against the fragmentation of meaning, the despair that one faces when confronted with the death of self, which is part of each person's life."

One hope in the search for meaning in elderescence is that we can find a way to end fragmentation, to find wholeness of meaning.

Gero-transcendence leaves the fragments behind, honoring a wholeness of feeling, a unity of elements and a new meaningfulness that could change the reality in which we all live!

Purpose

"We have to enlist the elders . . . to help and guide a crafting of new myths to reculturation." (Gutmann, *Reclaimed Powers*) A change in meaning leads to a change in how one responds to the events in one's life; meaning has intention and intention leads to action with purpose, borne of wisdom.

"It is weariness of all pursuits that creates weariness of life," spoke the wise Cicero. Many elderescents have the courage borne of purpose and have spoken about making the 'good fight,' and of having to be the ones who "get out in front of the bulldozers!"

"This brings me to the main thesis of this book," declared psychologist G. Stanley Hall in *Senescence*, "which is that intelligent and well-conserved aging have very important social and anthropological functions in the modern world not hitherto utilized or even recognized . . .This is marked by an Indian Summer of increased clarity and efficiency of intellectual work . . .The distraction from passion, lust for wealth and power . . . and place and fame, have abated and in their stead comes, normally, not only a philosophic calm but a desire to draw from accumulated experience and knowledge . . . lessons of life . . . all we have learned from the human comedy."

These are G. Stanley Hall's prophetic words spoken almost one hundred years ago, acknowledging the duty of an aging population to the future of humanity. Today, there is an increasing demand that the gifts one has to offer in later life not be squandered.

Throughout history the phrase *possessing wisdom* has often been used to honor the elderly, making the clear assumption that aging brings wisdom. Wisdom gives direction to purpose. Two thousand years ago, the Chinese philosopher and seer Confucius declared that after sixty, one could be wise enough to study the books of ancient wisdom. It has been said that wisdom cannot be taught, that it comes from an integration of knowledge and practical experience. Once one is aware of one's ego-driven needs and willing to manage them, an apprenticeship in the exploration of wisdom can begin.

In *Still Here*, Ram Dass writes, "Wisdom involves emptying and quieting the mind, an application of the heart and the alchemy of reason and feeling. In wisdom we are standing back viewing the whole, weighing meaning and contemplating."

Wisdom has been described as evolutionary in that it involves humankind's growth toward a divine meaning or a spiritual understanding. Wisdom entails acceptance, particularly an acceptance of life as it is, the ability to see with equanimity, and the ability to evaluate knowledge. Wisdom questions, creating a balance between knowing and doubting.

In *America, The Wise* (1998), Roszak says, "to become wise, examine your experience. When you are willing to grow up without fear that you are old you can give up the adult values that block wisdom . . . wisdom is seeing through illusions of youth."

Erickson defined wisdom as related to personal growth in older adulthood, explaining that it is the acceptance of life as one has lived it, along with an adaptation to physical deterioration and eventual death. Jung also speaks of wisdom in relationship to growth, noting that it is a progressive confrontation with the deep aspects of the self, including the unconscious, and integrates the dark side with the opposing internal forces, balancing good and evil.

Conscious aging, a phrase first coined by Jung fifty years ago, is now a spiritual movement established by an active contingent of elderescents. Jung wanted to bestow dignity and honor onto the process of aging as a spiritual quest. In 1990, building upon Jung's idea, Ram Dass delivered a lecture series, "Conscious Aging," in which he asserted that aging is painful if you believe you are simply your body or your personality. Today *conscious aging* has spread as a popular phrase signifying a process of becoming aware of one's existence, i.e., what one is feeling, thinking, and sensing, as well as an awareness of one's environment.

The Omega Institute, a well-known educational center in Rhinebeck, New York, has provided a home for the *conscious aging* movement for over a decade. They offer workshops and conferences in health, psychology, cultural arts, and spirituality, enabling participating elderescents to embark on creative and spiritual journeys that promise to be life-changing.

Rabbi Zalman Schachter has further expanded on this movement by organizing elderescents to engage in thoughtful work and dialogue through a process called *age-ing to sage-ing.* He said, "I wish for all of us to experience a conscious transit to the wider life." It was during Rabbi Schachter's own struggle to deal with mortality that he realized how much the elderescent has to offer society. When the reality of the inevitable physical aging is one's prime focus, a sense of despair and futility can pervade one's feeling of self-worth. "If you value your consciousness you can step aside from the awareness of the aging process and revel in the conscious experience, the awareness that is not going to die, it has no time limit. This inner awareness is power. This life stage is about completion, preparing for death, about transmitting wisdom into the culture, deepening one's connections and one's perspectives, and exploring the meaning of life. It is a tremendously new domain to map." (*Age-ing to Sage-ing)*

Rabbi Schachter views conscious aging as a process into which one grows, a process that leads one to a "harvesting of life . . . how you bring to fruition who you are and who you have become through life." In his teaching Schachter invites others in our society to embrace a paradigm shift in consciousness toward a positive image of aging, linking age with the "sage." Elders, he notes, have "distilled their life experience in such a way that their very presence becomes a witness to others. Originally this was what some tribal societies had; elders were a repository of wisdom and awareness, and younger people would check with them and say, 'Am I on the right track?' I like to use the word as a verb—eldering—because it's a process in a consciousness shift." *(Spiritual Eldering: A Conversation . . . Noetics: Connections)*

In 1995 the Omega Institute held a Circle of Elders gathering in which participants explored the aging experience through a change in consciousness. One elderescent reported, "They hung a velvet cloak around my shoulders and reviewed my life and honored it. I realized that I am not a human being having a spiritual experience but a spiritual being having a human experience." *Spiritual* is used in these contexts as that which is separate from the physical and material, and pertains to what some religions call 'soul life.'

Emerging from this conscious aging movement is the conviction that an awareness of aging by those experiencing it can provide society-at-large with a great resource: the wisdom of its elders.

Elderescents who are committed to the path of conscious aging have created two working models: finding new purpose in 'doing' through social consciousness, and finding new being through a spiritual quest. Maggie Kuhn and the Gray Panthers, Laura Huxley, and former president Jimmy Carter and his wife Rosalind all typify those individuals who found purpose in socially conscious activities. Those on a spiritual quest are exemplified by Jung's call for individuation and Schachter's process of spiritual eldering. Each path emphasizes *examined* experience and a state of mindful meditation and contemplation in the face of changes brought about by the aging process.

After being forced to retire at the age of sixty-five, Maggie Kuhn and six other women organized the Gray Panthers (1920) in what originally was an intergenerational effort to work on social issues and later the Vietnam War. Kuhn felt liberated as an older adult,—free to speak out, "to be really radical . . . I've set myself a goal to say something really outrageous every day and have outlived my opposition."

Kuhn offers elder Americans four roles she calls the Four M's: "Mentoring, Mediating, Monitoring, and Mobilizing for peace and ecology. One needs a passionate purpose—the rocking chair leisure world—what a waste! What a waste! We who have no risk to fear, we who have historical perspective, who can take the challenge of change. We ought to be leading the change, ought to be out of the rocking chairs—no more rocking chairs, no more leisure world."

In a speech before the Omega Conference in 1995, at the age of eighty-seven, Kuhn asked the audience to join with her in a Gray Panther exercise. "Open your eyes wide to keep watch on the world. Open your mouth to growl and shout at injustice. Open your arms to embrace all and shake your fists to get results."

Mobilizing the elderescent community to redefine themselves in a more positive way has caught fire over the last twenty years. In 1983 Robert Butler introduced the term *productive aging* to describe and support the valuable contributions that elderescents have been making in volunteer work. *Active aging* is a phrase the World Health Organization uses to focus on elderescent longevity and its impact on society.

At eighty-six Laura Huxley, wife of Aldous Huxley, focused her life's work on the needs of the children of the world through her organization, *Children: Our Ultimate Investment.* Her message is love; her teaching is straightforward. "This is who I am. I think that comes from the elders' point of view that the clock is running down in terms of earthly life and it is time to get things done and done well."

Zalman Schachter not only lives his life as a spiritual being but is also dedicated to social action, believing that elderescents' wisdom provides the "archetype, the myth, the paradigm, the script" to deal with aging. Schacter calls for a *togethering* to reshape and develop a new sense of aging. "We cannot deny that throughout history wise and generous elders have existed; however, the current generation of elders are the first to tackle aging on such a massive scale. We must have an answer to: How will I spend my last years without them being a drag on me and my loved ones?" His answer is to encourage elders to become mentors and writers. "Mentoring is the natural, holistic way of transmission . . . make a deposit of our earned life riches into our future account in the world bank of consciousness from which we are going to draw in the next incarnation."

For Schachter this process is not religious in the sense of being tied to a particular affiliation, but represents a development of spiritual consciousness. He speaks in *Spiritual Eldering* of the wise elder whose very presence conveys wisdom to the young. "When one sees oneself as a cell of the *global brain* then the purpose of life becomes clear. We are all part of this global brain. We take and we give back through mentoring. We take responsibility, give loving care and are connected to all. I look at this substance, the body, it's biological, it's organic . . . and someday it will get recycled." He continues, "It also contains experience and wisdom; if that were to die it would grieve me." Schachter speaks of God—not as the "Old Man" but "God as Verb, energizing the universe, God as Source of movement. Open yourselves to the Godding . . . [meaning full disclosure.] Open yourselves to the world; take down the barriers; drop the masks."

Schachter offers one model for conscious aging; there are others as varied as there are individuals. Jimmy Carter mediates for peace throughout the world; Colin Powell established programs for educating poor minorities and, more recently, as Secretary of State, acts as mediator in peace talks for the Bush administration. A number of former "first ladies" have fought to end illiteracy, drug addiction, and alcohol abuse, and artists like Pete Seeger, now in his eighties, continue to exemplify the human spirit through songs and social activism.

AARP's monthly magazine, *Modern Maturity,* profiles many little known elderescents. Organizations facilitating elderescent expression of a social consciousness number in the hundreds and are daily increasing. At eighty Mabel Clare proudly has provided food, education, health, and housing for the Mexican and American poor along the Texas border for over thirty years. A retired scientist educator Howard Heydt mentors school children in a unique program, ReSet, one of many volunteer project organizations. Volunteer Vacations combines elderescents' urge to give back with the desire to travel. Global Volunteers send people willing to cover their own travel expenses to other lands for three or more weeks to teach English, build needed infrastructure, and mentor good will. The Court Appointed Special Advocate Association is another unique program, which offers elderescents a chance to advocate for foster children in the judicial system.

The Jubilados Experiment: a Sangha of Conscious Aging, in Santa Fe, New Mexico, was an effort by elderescents to create a community in which conscious 'doing' and conscious 'being' were practiced. Their community was committed to a three-pronged effort combining meaning and 'doing' in a "contemplative practice, service to the community, and respect for the environment." The community, consisting of 120 people, two-thirds of whom were over sixty, sought a life built around a spiritual core. As they journeyed together through the process of conscious aging, as well as contributing to the community at large, they became a close-knit spiritual family.

As one member said, "This group differs from mainstream aging groups in that it is willing to do a dance back and forth between the ten thousand joys and ten thousand sorrows. It is willing to face the really tough stuff without becoming all gloom and doom but rather to figure out how to be with it wisely. At the same time, we are able to laugh and have a certain lightness and joyousness about aging." Another reported, "Even my children don't want to talk about my aging and dying. They are not interested. Nowhere have I found such a focus as we have here . . .We're simply showing who we are. It really feels like we're starting a movement that's going to change—or at least contribute to changing—the face of aging in our culture."

Purpose emerges from meaning, and meaning is further cultivated and expanded as beliefs are put into action. New observations and insights may also generate new meanings. Educating society and each other about the value of this new stage of life will enable elderescents to enhance the paradigm shift, bringing an appreciation of older people as valuable members of society with much to share.

Home, Hearth, and Family: The Changing Sense of Self and Relationships

Responding to a query about her plans on leaving her position as Secretary of State, Madeline Albright responded, "I am going to write my autobiography" and, adding with a smile, "My granddaughter, who knows me through TV and points to grandma in the news reports, will now have my lap on which to crawl."

In elderescence, home, family, and spouse become increasingly important. 'Nesting', finding a final place in which to settle, and/ or remaking one's home base, all became central. Renovating homes, building guest quarters, or possibly relocating may become joint projects. Perhaps (in anthropomorphic terms) as birds have been observed to prepare to settle in by picking and pulling as they build their nests, sitting and adjusting the shape, elderscents in the early stages do the same as they settle into their nests.

John Mosedale, the retired CBS reporter, writes in *The First Year: A Retirement Journal,* "I've been tackling the basic retirement job the past couple of weeks, cleaning out the garage. We don't have a garage so what I've been cleaning out is the room that is my study . . . "

With the shift in focus to home as one's world, some elderescents report becoming obsessed with home building and/ or renovation as they attempt to protect themselves against feelings of loss and emptiness. These projects can give them a temporary sense of having meaning in their lives. Busyness offers its own distraction, making it possible to deny loss, loss of structure, loss of meaning, and a greater sense of uncertainty about the future. The "betwixt and between" dynamic of denial is played out through the desire to find a place in which to rest, to be, and in which to prepare for whatever comes next.

In the words of one elderescent, "I moved back to the farmhouse and spent the first two months reestablishing it as my home . . . For those first months I don't think I sat on any of the sofas for more than moments at a time . . . " Another retired couple spent four years building first a guest house and then a unique main house, largely unaided by professional help. The completed project was exactly as they had fantasized, a fulfillment of their dreams, and yet, five years later they increasingly think of downsizing into something that would require less maintenance.

Homemaking activities may be seen as one's last opportunity to establish a perfect dwelling place, as in the dream house fantasized years ago, or as an expression of one's creativity, i.e., a home as a monument. Nesting activities may also be expressions of a desire for more freedom or control over one's environment, whether as a desire for more solitude, or for new interdependent communities. Some elders may seem self-indulgent and self-absorbed in their nesting activities, something that was never possible while fully employed and responsible for a growing family. However these activities are expressed, the settling in process is a transition from *doing* to *being*.

A retired teacher, Doreen, recounts her decision to retire in order to do everything she wanted. Her oft-repeated phrase was, "I am having the time of my life . . . I wanted my marital bedroom suite taken out of my bedroom. I got myself a four-poster bed, new rugs, a bidet and a grand piano. I got the three things I have always wanted; it is liberating, I tell you . . . It is such a wonderful feeling."

She remembers her misery living in a marriage that wasn't working. Though the divorce was difficult she finally began to know what she wanted. "I am free. I think that is the most important thing. Now I have it and I am happy as can be. I am free and so I intend to make the rest of my life count by doing everything I've always wanted to do! I don't know how long it is going to last."

Once 'nesting' is complete or in process, elderescents will face changes in their relationships, to family, adult children, grandchildren, friends, and to their spouses or partners. Work relationships may diminish, replaced by increased bonding with friends and family. "I would assume that happiness and contentment now depends on a multitude of factors . . . primarily interpersonal relationships," explained one elderescent.

Erickson identified two "pulls" on elderescents in the eighth stage of life, generativity or stagnation. Generativity refers to the essence of caring, nurturing, and maintaining the succeeding generations, i.e., sustaining the connections of self with a future that continues after death. It was Erickson's postulate that unless one became involved with the generative activities of caring for one's grandchildren, elderescents would stagnate. He later added the idea that generative activities could also involve artistic pursuits like painting, writing, mentoring, and creating other symbols of meaning that would live on after one's death. Telling one's story can certainly bequeath meaning to the next generations.

Erickson's last book *Vital Involvement in Old Age* (1986) made an imperative stand for elderescents to take active roles in their communities. Concern for our nation, our planet, a sense of social responsibility for all mankind, gives elderescents a purpose for their own survival. Generativity is seen as a cultural response to finitude and the culturally constructed sense of self.

Generativity is the secular form of self-transcendence, and can be viewed as a symbolic immortality! For Madeline Albright and many of the elderescents we interviewed, grandchildren and family are kept as a central focus. One elderescent clearly invested in family said, "The joys—in family life to be completely present . . . or nearly so! The opportunity to spend more time with children and grandchildren is celebrated. The freedom from responsibility has been exhilarating, an opportunity to enjoy my home, my children and grandchildren. I make family a priority. We can now offer additional support."

Another says, "I think of my presence in my kids' lives and want to be there when they have children of their own. I believe it is nice for kids to have parents in the background and also the same for my grandchildren when they are born."

In the compelling words of Florida Scott Maxwell in *Measure of My Days,* "I love my family for many reasons; for what I see them to be, for the loveliness they have been, for the good I know in them. I love their essence, their 'could be', and all this in spite of knowing their faults well. I love the individual life in them that I saw when in bud. I have spent much of my life watching it unfold, enchanted and anxious . . . No matter how old a mother is she watches her middle-aged children for signs of improvement. It could not be otherwise for she is impelled to know that the seeds of value sown in her have been winnowed. She never outgrows the burden of love, and to the end she carries the weight of hope for those she bore."

More elderescents today are assuming a larger responsibility in the care of grandchildren, either on a regular basis, freeing the parents for additional employment, or affording them time together. "Now I can go down to see my daughter and her family . . . We have a base now near our kids and grandkids . . . I have been able to spend quality time with my youngest son and his wife."

Caring for one's grandchildren was an accepted phenomenon, of course, when families always lived in proximity to each other and when life on the farm included several generations. Now, due to earlier retirement within the last decade or so, some grandparents have assumed a large portion of the care of their grandchildren as a "second career." Though some of these elderescent parents had reveled in the freedom from responsibility that a childless nest had afforded them, they returned to do their duty—a growing trend among baby boomers and their elderescent parents. Gutmann, as we noted earlier, has identified a desperate need for a return to the extended family in order to combat society's deculturation and the degradation of our cultural values.

In intimate conversations, however, some elderescents, while expressing a love for their grandchildren, also declare that they do not want the responsibility of raising another family. As one spoke with candor: "I'll take care of my grandchildren for a day or even a weekend but don't plan to come and live with me."

There is this subtle, often unexpressed feeling, that "this time is my time." The idea of a return to narcissism seems to contradict the clear message from Erickson that a commitment to generativity is essential for health in later life. The extremes of either position may be unhealthy choices. Rather, a balance between loving care and interest in one's children and grandchildren and an appreciation of the desire and need for one's own personal time is essential for a satisfying, healthy elderescence. To further complicate this analysis, the desire to care for grandchildren may be motivated by a feature of narcissism, i.e., "I need to impart or even indoctrinate my grandchildren with my values . . .They must do me proud!" All pursuits, undoubtedly, must be credited with a bit of narcissism.

This life stage affords time not only for one's grandchildren but time for one's own adult children as well, a unique opportunity to get to know them better as adults and spend time with them on an 'equal playing field.' Whether through helping care for grandchildren, or living in proximity to one's adult children, elderescents may develop true friendships with their adult offspring. Mutual respect and regard may develop through more frequent contact in which intimate thoughts, values, and aspirations are shared. Adult children may develop empathy for their elderescent parents as they exchange memories of family life; disappointments and misunderstandings disclosed between mature adults, have a chance for resolution. "Why did you do . . ?" or "What really happened when Grandpa Jones died. . . ?" are examples of the kinds of questions that may find resolution in adult dialogue, truly a gift of elderescence.

Elderescents have more time to share personal stories and reminiscing with friends and family helps them to connect with the younger generation. Stories may also help them feel more highly regarded. As the writer Rachel Remen states, "Everyone is a story . . . it is the way wisdom gets passed along . . . the stuff that helps us to live a life worth remembering . . . It comes not from any outer achievement but from the richness of experiencing life and sharing the inner experience of life with others."

The personal stories of our elders become part of the family legacy. Who will be interested in these stories, if not family and close friends?

Many elderescents also speak of the importance of maintaining friendships during this stage. There is time now to nurture longstanding relationships with friends and to reach out more fully to those friends in need, whether via long overdue correspondence or in actual visits.

The connections with both friends and family are a central form of protection against dwelling on one's losses. Many elders have lost contact with friends and colleagues from work, for example. One retired engineer says, "The loss of contact with old friends is turning out to be the only regretful part of retirement so far." The new emphasis on more time for family and friends is often conveyed with a sad note; indeed, because, during the primary part of many adults' lives, family and friends often took a back seat to work. One retiree remarks that retirement is the "first time I have lived in a community." This suggests the predominant, perhaps exclusive, place his profession once played in his life. Another speaks in a similar vein, "When I go to conventions now I don't 'convench' as hard as I used to . . . taking in all the sessions of interest—I spend time rather renewing old friendships."

The image of the elderescent who spends a lot of time alone has often been viewed as pathetic, lonely, and sad. However, a closer, multidimensional view of this later stage of life has given a new perspective and greater understanding, bringing about a shift in society's awareness of aging and a new appreciation of solitude as a reinvigorating and enjoyable experience. Solitude, indeed, does not necessarily imply loneliness. This point was made so emphatically by our interviewee Kathleen who said, "I do spend a lot of time alone, but I cherish it. I am not lonely!"

Paul Tillich speaks of the two aspects of spending time alone: loneliness and solitude. "Loneliness is the pain of being alone. Solitude, on the other hand, is the glory of being alone."

And yet, seeking alone time has never been, until perhaps recently, an approved behavior in our culture. Instead, "What have you been doing?" is often the refrain.

Florida Scott-Maxwell at eighty-six spoke to this point in her poignant book, *Measurement of My Days,* "I wonder if living alone makes one more alive. No precious energy goes in disagreement or compromise. No need to augment others, there is just yourself, just truth—a morsel—and you. You went through those long years when it was a pain to be alone, now you have come out on the good side of that severe discipline. Alone you have your own way all day long, and you become very natural. Perhaps this naturalness extends into heights and depths, going further than we know; as we cannot voice it we must just treasure it as the life that enriches our days . . . Although I am absorbed in myself, a large part of me is constantly occupied with other people. I carry the thought of some almost as a baby too poorly to be laid down . . . I dwell on their troubles, their qualities, their possibilities as though I kept them safe by so doing."

These experiences of solitude, often cherished, are corroborated by many female elderescents, although they also report that being alone can be painful, causing anxiety and self-doubt. In particular, those elderescents facing the loss of family members and friends may be plagued by thoughts about why they are still "here," especially if they have few spiritual connections or lack the comfort of a religion or it's community. As noted earlier, without a central meaning for life, sadness over one's losses can turn to despair and even a wish to end life altogether.

A predominant belief in the Western world is that some kind of attachment to others, to a God, or to an ideal, is essential for well-being. In the East, however, Buddhism and Hinduism stress the opposite— detachment is regarded as the key to peace and serenity, which is found in an acceptance of universal unity or oneness. In the West, religion as embodied in a church or synagogue can be important in many elderescents' lives, a place in which they experience a connection to something larger than themselves. For the religious elderescent comfort comes from "spiritual growth that transforms the loneliness into a creative solitude imbued with the knowledge that even aloneness into the valley of the shadow of death does not separate one from God." (Payne, B & McFadden, S. *Aging and the Religious Dimension)*

A journey to self-knowledge and meaning is essential to elderescents in facing his/ her new life. In the words of Clark Moustakas, "The lonely experience can give a person back to himself, affirm his identity, and enable him to take steps toward new life . . . Love has no meaning without loneliness; loneliness becomes real only as a response to love." As Florida Scott-Maxwell notes, "Solitude can be glorious." She adds, "Old people can seldom say 'we' . . . The habit of thinking in terms of 'we' goes; . . . we become I . . . My kitchen linoleum is so black and shiny that I waltz while I wait for the kettle to boil. This pleasure is for the old who live alone. The others must vanish into their expected roles." (*Measure of My Days)*

With the focus shifting to home and family, many elderescents experience increased attention to their relationship with a spouse or primary partner, bringing about some new challenges. Orchestrating unstructured schedules with spouses or partners can be daunting, particularly when there is a new need for more personal freedom. The pull toward togetherness, similar to a "honeymoon" phase, can be a powerful force as well. The differing needs of partners around these issues often initiates struggles and requires compromise. One elderescent offers, "I face a pull toward total togetherness—twenty-four-hour intimacy—and another pull toward wanting a solitary journey into hermitage. Some of the time I like that there are just two of us; sometimes this is hard, dealing with his moods. I can do whatever I want; but isn't it a balance between my need to search within and my enjoyment to be in this world, active and with others . . . I want to explore my inner world but at times it has seemed hard. There are detractors—my husband calls out. "Do you want to go . . . ?"

Another elderescent writes, "Retirement has brought about noticeable changes in my interaction with my wife. We have both experienced frustrations in adjusting to one another's schedules or more accurately my lack of one, which has cramped her usual schedule of interests and activities. She has found our more frequent travel a mixed blessing, wanting on the one hand to continue her regular routine but also enjoying the trips. I, of course, have been irritated by her not dropping everything at a moment's notice."

Some male elderescents sensitively acknowledged the effects their retirement has had on their homemaker wives. "I realize that my wife does not retire, she maintains her domestic chores. We need to monitor our face-to-face daily contact so I spend the morning in my study." Another says, "My wife and I have an excellent relationship, and I've tried not to let my retirement negatively influence her valued activities in the church and with her friends. We both cherish our four children and seven grandchildren, one incentive to fixing up the house to provide space for clan gatherings several times a year."

Mosedale, in *The Retirement Journal*, offers these general insights on relationships after retirement: "Contrary to myth, I think that probably for most couples in retirement, the best part is that retirement gives them more time to be together. There are many more happy couples than you might guess from what you read and hear . . . Betty and I had traveled 1,851 miles on our trip back from the island (a summer retreat in Wisconsin) but, in this first summer of my retirement, we have traveled a greater distance than that, beyond sickness and death, past the imagined obstacles of idle time into an understanding that however much time we have left together, Betty and I, it will not be time enough."

Twenty-Four-Hour Togetherness

Examining the day-to-day lives of two elderescent couples presents a picture of the changes some experience during this phase of life. Peter and Sarah's story is typical.

After thirty years, Peter retired from his primary occupation as a scientist, five years before his wife Sarah decided to leave her profession. He spent the first year of his retirement recovering from heart surgery, writing about the experience while regaining his health and enjoying the morning talk shows that he had missed due to his early work schedule. Toward the end of that year, Peter began to think about what he wanted to do with the rest of his life. Not inclined toward 'handy man' jobs, he decided to seek part-time work as a consultant. As a result of his reputation at the National Institute, Peter felt he would not have a hard time contacting contractors. He soon found that his new employers were more interested in the contacts and inside information he could provide than in his knowledge. Peter further found that after thirty years in a top advisory and research position, adjusting to new company policies and new employees was difficult and demeaning. This propelled him into exploring volunteer opportunities.

Sarah, relieved that her husband had had a complete recovery from heart surgery, wanted to focus on her own work. She hoped Peter would soon find something that would make him happier, since volunteering had become problematic, and he'd begun experiencing bouts of depression. Luckily, one of Peter's former colleagues presented him with an offer to help on a research project two to three days a week, an outgrowth of a previous project that Peter had been involved in at his former work place.

Peter began to travel, write, and conduct interviews as part of his new position, where he was also in contact with colleagues from the 'old days.' This began a good period for the couple, whose children had all 'left the nest.' Sarah began to assume less responsibility in her job and her hours became more flexible. Occasionally she traveled with Peter, particularly if the trip afforded them an opportunity to visit their children.

For three years this schedule seemed to work. Peter felt that his expertise was still of value to his company, and, with less on-the-job pressure and responsibility, he had time to ride his tractor and perform odd jobs around the house. When Peter's project ended in success, the issue of 'what next' loomed again.

Sarah had begun to consider retirement herself. With her husband back at home, at 'loose ends' and dissatisfied, she felt pressured to make their lives pleasurable. The emptiness in Peter's life was causing him to withdraw, and he was becoming more dependent and passive.

After a renewed search for volunteer work, Peter found a mentoring program in the local school system, in which he would work with individual students needing extra help in science. Because the work called upon his scientific training, it helped him to feel useful again.

Five years after Peter's retirement Sarah retired and a new set of dynamics emerged. Throughout their marriage Peter and Sarah had been largely home focused except for their professions. Outside activities were usually done together and rearing four children was a shared commitment. Neither Peter nor Sarah enjoyed hobbies, so the transition to structuring those open hours was not familiar to them.

Now Peter had a companion but all was not bliss. He had settled into retirement, transitioning into a life without constant, consuming professional demands, and adjusting to the loss of the attendant rewards of work well done. Now Sarah had entered the first phase of the retirement transition, and, once again, they were not in sync. If they could maintain the feeling that they were on vacation, enjoying a holiday, they could play and enjoy each other, since their recreational choices had always been compatible.

While Peter had worked through the losses that come with retirement, Sarah was now struggling with the feeling of having no purpose, and no overriding focus in her life.

Like many other couples, Peter and Sarah tended to indulge their unhappiness by complaining about each other. Each wanted the other to solve what they really needed to resolve within themselves. When Peter became depressed, Sarah would think about leaving. When they both look back to those days now, they agree that there seemed to be a cyclical rhythm to their struggles. One day life was good and the next day one or the other or both were unhappy. They had once fantasized about total togetherness but now they were wondering if it was possible. They had to reconsider their patterns, their emerging wishes for time alone, for example.

Peter found a solution in running long errands and continuing the volunteer work that he found so satisfying, and a source of renewed energy and love.

Sarah tried to deny her need for time alone until overcome by annoyance or anger, causing conflict between them or serving to drive Peter away. Sarah, the type of person who found renewal and energy in exchanges with colleagues, needed time to regroup from the loss of a rewarding public life that had stroked her ego. Floundering, but having trouble acknowledging it, Sarah needed to explore new avenues of self-expression, and a way to recover a lost sense of personal meaning. Reflecting on past pursuits, she began thinking of revisiting her love of painting. She found that when she allowed herself time to pursue art, she often emerged gratified and radiant.

Sarah and Peter's twenty-four hour togetherness gave them time to know each other in ways that had never before been revealed, some fulfilling, some not. Because of the constancy of their connection, there was an opportunity for issues that were hurtful or painful to be worked out, not left to smolder.

The Creaks and Pains of Aging

The following story portrays another elderescent couple's adjustment to this new life stage. One morning Harry shared a revelation with his wife Rebecca that, until then, he had not been able to face. He hesitantly explained that in the morning, nestled in bed beside his wife, he felt open and engaged. Upon rising, however, as he confronted the obvious pain and discomfort of the effects of aging on his body and looked in the mirror as he dressed, fear gripped him. He constricted with anxiety, afraid that death might be at hand, or a potential disabling illness that could make life a living death.

Harry knows he may have ten more good years—or one—but the time he now has left seems more limited than ever before. Rarely does one contemplate death at age twenty, thirty, forty, or fifty. Rebecca realizes she cannot tell her husband that he is in good health, and not to worry. She knows he has to confront this challenge on his own. After confiding his feelings to his wife, Harry soberly remarked, "I will have to think about this and really deal with it."

Their sharing process led to a new understanding between them; that encouraged compassion and thus compromise and resolution. Peter and Sarah and Harry and Rebecca each continue on the journey to understand and know themselves and each other, a journey that is at times exciting and immensely satisfying, similar in ways to the experience newlyweds face as they learn to adjust to each other for the first time.

Elderescents often must confront the aging process and the prospect of mortality without the distraction of work and raising children. For some, it is the time when they meet and know their authentic selves. Margaret Freydburg so eloquently describes her process of confronting her mortality in *Growing Up In Old Age*. This process requires patience on the part of spouses or partners, and a commitment not to give up on what often has been a loving, long life together.

In *Grown-Up Marriage*, Judith Viorst offers, "Many of us, having benefited from a leap in life expectancy, will have lots of later years to spend with our spouse . . . 'Grow old along with me! The best is yet to be' can only evoke a skeptical 'Yeah, right!' . . . But growing older together instead of separately, and holding each other's hand as we make the trip, can be—if not the best life has to offer—a good deal better than going it alone."

For many elderescent couples, diminishing sexual ardor is another issue requiring attention in order to prevent misunderstandings and hurt feelings. Love may continue to grow but sexual passion is often diminished. As one elderescent confided, "Sex is something now one has to make an effort to arrange or deliberately orchestrate."

At seventy-three Jeanne Moreau, the "femme fatale" of the French movie scene, shared her thoughts on the subject of passion in later life with Mike Wallace on TV's "60 Minutes." Moreau, who in January 2001 became the first woman inducted into the French Academy of Fine Arts, still commands the acclaim and the attention of adoring fans as she did at thirty-five years of age. Moreau continues to work, making two or three movies each year, as well as TV appearances. In reference to her two marriages and several notable affairs, she said, "That is what life is about . . . nothing lasts."

When asked about the pervading view in this country, that passion in a woman of a certain age is unseemly, she replied, "They are right!" She explained, "Oh, come on, passion . . . when you get to be sixty . . . you know about love, but love is not passion. I would hate to be still overcome with passion." She added that, for her, love deepens with age while passion is waning.

Other elderescents have agreed, stating that love, which transcends fleeting physical attractions, is preferable to passion as one is aging. More important than passion is how your partner feels and how well you get along. A loving companionship in elderescence will always enjoy gentle physical/ sexual moments.

Moreau's attitude about aging and its physical changes merge with her beliefs about sexual passion. In speaking about how other actresses have faded from the movie scene after aging, she said, "They have to worry about their cheek bones, about their neck and carry the image of eternal youth." In contrast, she said, "I love life. I love freedom. I have no vanity. Just because there are a few wrinkles . . . it's what goes on inside. I don't mind wrinkles. I mind what comes forward, what comes forth: anxiety, greed and resentment. It's a face that shows curiosity, look at that face, what is happening there, it moves on, that's what life is about."

For elderescents in intimate relationships much rests on the resolution of conflicts, particularly since they are more dependent upon their partners than at any other phase of life (even than at the old-old stage).

This can be a source of great anxiety and fear. As one elderescent describes, "If I were to become crippled, have a sudden heart failure, or lose mental capacity, would my spouse be able to take care of me?" Her chief concern was not about whether he would care for her but about whether he would do it the way she wanted, with sensitivity to her needs.

Intimacy need not breed contempt if focusing on one's own process is open to review by both parties. Being aware of how we project feelings and needs onto others is essential when living intimately with another. The adolescent uses projection to externalize the negative feelings, to protect a tender sense of identity on the journey to self-acceptance. Elderescents, however, must 'own' their projections, i.e., the negative images of self, on their journeys toward greater authenticity, integrity, and self-knowledge. Lack of self-awareness can result in 'dumping' on one's partner, and endless bickering. Or as Judith Viorst notes, "mens' problems very often become their wife's problems."

Increased intimacy in elderescence calls for a continuing process of growth, one of self-exploration, self-acceptance, and honest self-expression.

There is sagacity in learning to accept differences and to compromise within any relationship, but especially at this stage of life. When one has put thirty, fifty, or sixty years into a relationship one usually realizes that to give up that history, that love, along with the opportunity to continue to grow would be absurd. Maturity encourages further development of one's patience, along with self-confrontation, and acceptance of one's mortality. The wisdom borne of perspective leads many elderescent couples into a union of deep friendship and compassion that may not have been as fully enjoyed until this time.

Society has yet to comprehend the difficult changes that impinge on an elderescent marriage or union. Beginning in the initial stage of elderescence, couples must address the changes in personal status each partner experiences as a result of retirement, new-found freedom, unstructured time, negotiation of personal space, and struggles with identity. These changes require an awareness of the hazards faced during this time and their possible effects on each partner. Some elderescents will need professional help, or some other means of support, in learning to express their thoughts and feelings as they go through these changes.

The grim possibility of the death of one member of a couple, more likely than at any stage prior to elderescence, hangs overhead. Each elderescent has to accept their own death before this stage can be lived fully, and the mortality of one's spouse or partner should be planned for and accepted as inevitable as well. Whether a couple has been in love or not, the loss of a partner produces a profound sense of loss and loneliness, alleviated only by time and softened by connection with close friends and family. Some widows we interviewed shared that they still talk to the deceased husband to maintain a sense of the closeness they once had. Bereaved elders who are religious or spiritually inclined may find comfort in the belief that someday they will be with their loved one. If care giving has been of long duration and demanding, the remaining spouse may feel ambiguous about the death of a loved one, particularly if he or she was in pain or demented. Long-term care giving brings with it not only the looming loss of one's life companion but also the added burden of daily tasks normally handled by the person now ill.

After a period of mourning, elderescent widows, widowers, and partners who have a strong sense of self and have accepted their own mortality will be able to resume active lives, whether in returning to work or in maintaining a social network of friends and family. The loss may also be a stimulus for a new consciousness to emerge. As reported by some we interviewed, there follows a journey into self-transcendence or a new sense of a cosmic universe, with religious, spiritual, or secular community connections providing continued meaning and purpose.

In her book *Growing up In Old Age*, Margaret Freydburg addresses these aspects of widowhood: "I must accept as irreversible that loneliness caused by the disappearance of the sustaining presence of the person I was closest to in the world—in one sense the closeness of male and female union, in another sense of friendship and mutual dependencies . . . The consequences of being left alone are hard . . . being precipitated with horrible abruptness into the sole management, hitherto shared by two, of everything that had to do with material existence."

It has been said that the older you become, the more obsessed you become with yourself. We return to Gutmann's notion of narcissism in *Reclaimed Powers*. "As the social structure is dismantled, narcissism again becomes available to the post-parental self . . . that fund of narcissism can become the basis of new self-realizations or recruited to the formation of new, more extensive social bonds."

This development must be seen from two perspectives. First, self-absorption and self-reflection are necessary in order to claim or reclaim the authentic self, thus to achieve new meaning in this stage of life. Too much 'time on one's hands,' however, can be fresh ground for the cultivation of narcissism and self-centeredness. "I must have time to live my own life," says one retiree, having felt for all her life responsive to another's needs. "I enjoyed the solitude, doing whatever I felt like whenever I felt like it." The danger in this second perspective is that a self-centered lifestyle may result in isolation and a sense of meaninglessness. Some elderescents verbalize the feeling that this new stage sends a signal that here is a chance to really live the wishes of adolescence, those dreams of "doing any damn thing we want when we want." In *Seasons of a Woman's Life*, Daniel Levinson suggests that vital adolescing may be done as one seeks to have fuller meaning in one's life.

Gutmann reiterates these ideas: "With the phasing out of the parental emergency, fathers and mothers have less need to live within the altruistic conjugal mode. The child is safely launched. In the post-parental years, adults finish paying their species dues. They no longer have to meet the psychological tax that is levied on our species. Having raised the next generation of viable and procreant children, the parents have earned the right to be again, at least in token ways, omnipotential . . .They can afford the luxury of elaborating the potentials and pleasures that they had to relinquish in service of their parental task."

As we noted in an earlier section, the narcissism of adolescence or young adulthood is a self-focused stage of growth. During the procreation stage it is transformed to an external focus on one's offspring. In the post-procreation stage of later life, the focus on one's self returns, possibly in an attempt to obtain or construct a new sense of self and meaning for one's life.

These ideas appear to be consistent with the views of elderescent women we interviewed who talk about relishing the idea of "putting themselves first for a change." A natural, perhaps inborn, maternalism may temper the "me first" urge, however, if family should call upon them in need. Perhaps the joy in feeling needed again may obscure the need to put one's self first, at least for a time. One elderescent suggests this: "For the first time in my entire life, I'm not marching in anyone else's parade." But she also noted she was very willing "to arrange my time to help my younger daughter."

Perhaps many elderscents can achieve a balance between always being the "emeritus parent" and protecting one's boundaries. For elderescent men in folk cultures the return to narcissism is converted into the worship of the gods. In the Druze culture, for example, in Syria and Lebanon, Allah becomes the focus of everything and identification with him is fostered, sublimating the otherwise likely tendency to narcissism.

In 1933 Jung reported in *Modern Man in Search of a Soul*, "that men in later life become more passive and women become more assertive and aggressive. We might compare masculinity and femininity and their psychic components to a definite store of substances of which in the first half of life unequal use is made. A man consumes his large supply of masculine substance and has left over only the smaller amounts of feminine substance, which must now be put to use. Conversely, the woman allows her hitherto unused supply of masculinity to become active. This change is even more noticeable in the psychic realm than the physical . . . very often these changes are accompanied by all sorts of catastrophes in marriage, for it is not hard to discover what will happen when the husband discovers tender feelings and the wife her sharpness of mind."

Jung identifies the elderescent man as "more sensual, affiliative, dependent, hedonic, in effect, showing some femininity that was repressed during the procreation period." The elderescent woman becomes "more domineering, independent, unsentimental, and self-directed, asserting their own desires. They repossess the aggressive masculinity that they once lived out vicariously."

Though Gutmann in *Reclaimed Powers*, disagrees with Jung's notion of "masculinity and femininity substances" he affirms Jung's clinical observations (i.e. the tender feelings in the man and the wife's sharpness of mind.) They both assert that the passivity of the elderescent man and conversely the surfacing of masculinity in the elderescent woman can be a factor that causes disruption in later life marriages. Women begin marriages in dependent "Passive Mastery" and in later years assume an "Active Mastery."

In a study done in 1992 of 150 families in Parkville Illinois, Professor Margaret Huyck reported that elderescent men evidenced "gender expansion." She observed that they became more nurturing, while elderescent women become more assertive, sometimes the cause of "psychological distress," as was true for Peter and Sarah, a couple described earlier in this section. Unaware that this is a normal shift in the psychological characteristics of men and women in elderescence, a spouse can misinterpret the changes in his or her partner. Sarah worried about these changes in Peter. She became critical and nagging. Peter, on the other hand, felt demeaned by his emerging passivity and dependency.

These significant changes demand understanding and acknowledgement on the part of elderescents to ensure the well-being and survival of their partnerships and marriages. We have, in this culture, tended to shy away from identifying this 'crossover' phenomenon. The 'henpecked' husband is the butt of frequent jokes but questions remain as to what really happens when elderescent men retire; do they become 'domesticated' by virtue of being at home much of the time, or are they victims of a partner's proddings to take over the chores on the home front?

An elderescent wife says, "I worry as to what is happening to my husband. He is getting so passive, waits for me to orchestrate activities, and conversation. Sometimes he seems so passive or compliant that I wonder if he is 'losing it.'"

An elderescent husband comments, "The issue with my wife is that she wants me to cook and if I don't she is not happy." This is a man who retired at sixty-five years of age, has had serious medical problems for over ten years, and now leads a quiet life in which his schedule is his own and his activities include writing fiction, doing errands, and learning to play the piano. His wife, on the other hand, has resumed her work as an artist with intense enthusiasm, and resents the interference of housework and cooking.

Notable are the number of wives who seem to have taken over the managerial role on the home scene, and who are now 'running the show.' Some couples complain and feel anxious about these changes. Also, retirement causes a number of elderescent men to retreat or withdraw, perhaps because their roles in the world outside of the home have been diminished. Some become depressed, hedonic, irritable, or just feel lost. Alerting elderescents to the normalcy of these changes can provide relief and make these changes much easier. This does not suggest, however, that changes of this nature will not create tension; it takes acknowledging and 'working through' these changes to understand and accept each other.

Gutmann offers interesting analyses of changes in style and subject matter in the aging artist in *Reclaimed Powers.* In Picasso's final paintings he fuses the male and female together. In the Baiser (Kiss) paintings, for example, "The male and female is pressed together, joined by a common mouth. In this frantic clinging, limbs and parts lose their gender."

In a study of two New Yorker cartoonists, George Price and William Steig, Gutmann delineates what he calls "intra-psychic shifts in their drawings as they aged. Price's early cartoon themes invariably depicted a little boy who wants to be tough, courageous, and like the "big guys." In mid-life Price depicted characters who were less assertive in their struggles; he disparaged masculine qualities by poking fun at men who 'made it' in the male world. In his sixties and seventies, Price focuses on portraying Venus besieged by an adoring man trying to please a 'good mother' but never succeeding.

Steig initially focused on the masculine character but in his sixties and seventies, Steig seldom portrayed his 'World of Men,' instead he focused on the relationship between men and women. Women were usually drawn as dominant in the domestic setting. The shrewish wife was often depicted as badgering the passive man. In one cartoon, the male wore a tee shirt that said, "Flight;" the female tee shirt said, "Fight."

Gutmann's analysis of Georgia O'Keefe's paintings suggests that until she was forty-five, O'Keefe painted "a mouse-eyed view of the world, a tight focus, close-up details of flower portraits and shells." After age fifty-five she stopped painting flowers and painted vast spaces, rocky mountains, and dry sands.

Gutmann's view is that older male artists give up the hard-edged paintings of their youth as they age and Georgia O'Keefe moved in the other direction as she aged, from the "diffuse, pulsing colors" of her early flower paintings to the "sharp contours of mesa and narrowing road" of her elderescence. This change in style and focus may identify a new sense of self and personal meaning. Gutmann's message is that the inner psychological changes, the masculine/ feminine "sex role turnover" that occurs in the aging male and female population at large is also evident in the art productions of the aging artist.

Profound personality changes do occur in elderescence, clearly impacting both one's relationships and one's vulnerability to emotional disorders. Some elderescents acquire increased coping strategies, patience, and wisdom as a result of living through these changes. They are able to discover practical solutions to the vicissitudes of daily living. But for elderescents who are unable to accept the changes in personal status, and who are unable to deal with the complexities of emotion during this stage, life can be extremely precarious. Those who remain egocentric and self-absorbed as they attempt to deal with the inevitable losses that occur during this stage are more likely to experience emotional disorders.

Feelings of depression may occur as elderescents face both change and loss. Robert Butler, in his Pulitzer Prize winning book *Why Survive?* says, "Older persons (identified as sixty-five years and older) experience more stresses than any other age group, and these stresses are often devastating." Chronic depression may be a continuing reality for some.

For two elderescents we interviewed, a common personal theme was, "I feel I am always falling short." Though both had been successful professionals they seemed to lack an acceptance of their life as being valuable, leaving them both with the over-riding question: "Has my life made a difference?" They both acknowledged that in adolescence they first began to feel they did not 'measure up.' There was a lack of connection to a new lovable emerging self that could engender a feeling of 'goodness' in them. As Jung and others have suggested, the unfinished business of adolescence might be revisited in this later stage of life. One was a highly regarded and successful physician and spoke of the joys of retirement: "I loved not getting up in the morning, loved the release from so much responsibility, but what crept in was a sense of needing to do something worthwhile. I guess I am a Puritan at heart."

Adjusting to life after a serious illness can also bring up these feelings, as one elderescent noted: "I feel very out of the swim of things now." Another, who had sought help through psychotherapy, shared his mantra, "reconcile that the unfinished business is not going to get finished."

The ultimate "unfinished business" of accepting one's eventual death is often unresolved. One elderescent, in offering his intimate thoughts, described attending his family church but felt the acceptance of a "God image" as problematic. He seemed to want a connection to a higher power but was intellectually unable to accept this on faith.

For each of these very candid elderescents music was honored as a source of connection. It is interesting to note that many elderescents found music as a stimulus to their deep soulful feelings, as well as to a *force* beyond themselves.

As noted by Gutmann in the second edition of *Reclaimed Powers* an in-depth look at the clinical psychology of later life, severe psychological conditions may emerge as an individual attempts to overcome a sense of depletion and obsolescence. Some elderescents may exhibit signs of paranoia and delusional thinking as a way to defend against accepting the changing reality. "In a real sense, psychosis in later life represents a hectic attempt to conjure up the sources of self-esteem that are routinely supplied to traditional elders by a strong culture."

Loss of one's base of self-esteem may indeed be the source of the elderescent male's passivity and depression. Alzheimer's disease, which is on the increase, may also be accelerated in part by despair and the desire to be taken care of, a dependency that most individuals are incapable of acknowledging. In addition, psychosomatic symptoms may also develop as a way of masking the neediness of someone who is depressed. These defense mechanisms may often cover the essential pain and lack of meaning in an elderescent's life, and stand as a powerful motivator to encourage elderescents to apply themselves to the task of finding new meaning for this stage of life.

As mentioned earlier, elderescent men manage better in traditional folk cultures in which passivity and humility, or "passive mastery," facilitate their roles as culture-tenders. In essence, they become the norm bearers, responsible for passing the values, cultural rituals, and the rites of passage on to younger men. In our modern materialistic society we have no culture tenders. Elderescent men are given few roles or positions of authority as they age, in sharp contrast to the agrarian age, when they once held positions of honor until death. Stories from Biblical times describe two ancient kings, Oedipus and David, who rose from decline and depressive "sickness" to influence their people at times of great crisis. Were they spiritually invigorated by expectations that they serve the Divine by saving their nations? Surely this realization caused them, even in their eighties, to reengage in life.

Elderescents can serve the community in another important way— that of 'bearing witness' to what the younger generation is doing. In the role of the'audience,' elderescents serve as reviewers of current plays, concerts, and various other cultural activities in their communities. As observers, they see, listen, and can transmit to the younger generations their interpretations of current activities and events, tempered by the wisdom and perspective of a long-lived life. Elderescents need to establish a collective voice that can transmit their interpretations and analyses. In some communities they are doing this.

A group of elders over sixty years of age, some retired, some not, can be a formidable force in any decision-making issue. This was noted recently in our own small community. Two meetings were held to discuss whether to allow 200 acres of forest land to be purchased by a developer for construction of a golf course. Two meetings were held; one in the evening where the vote to 'approve' was slightly over 50%; another meeting was held at 12:00 noon. This meeting was a sea of white haired citizens all of whom overwhelming voted to deny the golf course plans. At the noon meeting many elderescents rose to speak from their hearts with authority and conviction about the issues of water conservation and potential toxic pollution. They wanted their community to retain its open spaces and its quality of serenity. The growing power of older citizens is a recent phenomenon attracting attention and respect in the business and political arenas. Perhaps, as Chinen has suggested, they can also be mediators in these conflicts of interest.

As we have previously suggested, though elderescents live a variety of different lifestyles, there seems to be a common quest for something greater than material possessions, for values other than consumerism. Free from striving hard for success, they have time for reflection on life's meaning, on the deep and profound moments that make it worthwhile. Without verbosity or display, elderescents are making their mark by creating models by which to live in this extended period of life and inventing new roles in which to find fulfillment.

As elderescents have testified in our interviews, finding and fixing up a home, spending time with the family, and staying involved in one's community can all help the elderescent to feel useful, but may not leave energy for the elderescent's deep inner journey toward the Self. As G. Stanley Hall remarks poignantly, serving to remind us all of his important message: In aging, "a new noetic or meditative urge emerges from the primal sources of all vital energy and gives new and deeper sense to life." (*Senescence*)

This is the gift of this stage of life.

Part Four

Our Reflections

ACKNOWLEDGING IMPERMANENCE
IN ELDERESCENCE

Change is a paramount theme in our story of elderescence. Change confronts, frightens, disarms, weakens, and delights us. In elderescence change accelerates. We eventually have to acknowledge that we cannot stop our bodies from changing or our experience of life itself from changing. Becoming absorbed in one's physical maladies and clinging to medical interventions or health remedies may give one the illusion that change can be stopped. Yet, when we pay attention to our experiences, our thoughts, our emotions, our desires, we will recognize the constant rhythm of change. We will have to accept that the aging process cannot be stopped and death is a reality we all must face.

In her book, *Composing a Life*, Margaret Bateson, the daughter of Margaret Mead, offers a perspective for understanding the effect of change in an elderescent's life. "The older person continues at some level in an active process of restructuring meaning to cushion the effect of major changes in form."

Elderescents, like people of all ages, seek a 'place to rest', to experience a sense of security and comfort. Some will say, "this will be our last move", alluding to the desire to have a permanent home. However, the transitory nature of experience inevitably creates anxiety. The changes for many elderescents are dramatic and assaultive to one's sense of stability. It is in elderescence that the reality of change must finally be acknowledged.

Some elderescents seek a sense of permanence in a faith that gives credence to life after death. Some seek immortality in the idea of living on through one's progenies. Creative activities can provide others the hope that they can live on through their work. One authors a book, which will carry his or her name. Another establishes a business; another erects a building bearing his or her name that remains for many decades. Mentoring passes on to others wisdom and compassion, touching the lives of many for years to come. Yet, all things, even those solidified over time by habitual thinking, will change and eventually cease to exist. Change is the only thing that we can know or count on for sure.

An essential task in this new stage of life is to learn to live with the reality of one's own impermanence, the impermanence of love relationships, of the natural world, and of society as we know it. Joseph Goldstein, a Buddhist scholar and teacher offers, "It may be simply an act of surrender. When I can experience impermanence fully, the image that often comes to mind is that of white-water rafting. My response to the danger seems to be either panic and holding on, or surrender. After rafting through enough rapids, I develop the faith or confidence to surrender, to let go."

A false sense of control or a belief in permanence often results in clutching to one's life, resisting change, which ultimately limits one's freedom of choice. In contrast, knowing and accepting impermanence is like a gateway for the heart and mind, which can then open to a liberating freedom. The reality of impermanence makes everything possible. William Blake speaks of this.

> He who binds himself to a joy
> doth the winged life destroy.
> But he who kisses the joy as it flies
> lives in eternal Sunrise.

The concept of impermanence is so obvious and yet our natural inclination is to deny that our lives on earth some day will end. It is the acceptance of the impermanence of all things that will eventually afford the elderescent a sense of *knowing* and thus personal stability.

Elderescence and the last stage of life, old, old age, are the only periods of life with clearly limited futures. Dealing with this limitation may give the elderescent a sense of immediacy, of the present, of the 'now.' Life can become more significant, as each moment is precious and responsibility for one's self becomes undeniable. In other stages of life we can easily deny the task of self-review for there is much to do and many 'ladders to climb.' To face the fact of impermanence and to grow in that reality, one must turn inward to one's unique self to find peace and serenity.

Elderescence offers the last time to ask, "Who am I?" In this search one may go through a process of life review, grieving one's losses, acknowledging with gratitude one's experiences, and come to an understanding of the cycle of life, and a sense of connectedness to one's history. The answer to "Who am I?" may simply be, "I am who I am."

Life is impermanent and impermanence, paradoxically, is permanent. Acceptance of this paradox can offer elderescents a new kind of engagement with life, a life lived more freely. Many we interviewed expressed an intense desire to finally find freedom, 'freedom from' and then 'freedom to' be themselves. In the words of an elderescent who has begun to accept impermanence, "I find that the concepts of impermanence and nonattachment are at the very center of my inner journey. I've had a heart attack, there are moments of feeling it's okay, life is temporary and we are not going to change that; the issue for me is to continue to work with how I go and the process of letting go. Impermanence has made my life much more significant . . . because so much of the time I have pushed away the fact that I'm dying."

Many of our elderescents have had unique experiences that have helped them reach wise insights about the nature of life. Acceptance of the impermanence of life and the acceptance of the end of one's life on earth have brought them a deeper sense of peace and completeness. This acceptance has led some elderescents to speak of a natural oneness, a universe that is limitless and life as limitless. Another word for limitlessness is abundance. If we can understand that our universe, and our cosmos is limitless and that life is ever evolving, that it too is limitless, we can understand life as ever abundant. Accepting impermanence, acknowledging the changing, evolving nature of all living beings, can release us from the fear of our own inevitable changes, and gives us equanimity and a sense of universal connectedness. Echoing the words of physicist David Bohm, who describes a continual process of the unfolding and enfolding of all things, Marcia Rose, a visual artist and teacher, writes, "The acceptance of change, of the forming and unforming, of the birth and the death, is actually truly the acceptance of life."

This gift of longevity is the elderescents' opportunity and our hope for new visions about life's meaning.

IN REVIEW

What have we revealed about this gift of longevity? First, it is undoubtedly here to stay. It is a reality of our human development and part of the dramatic evolution of life patterns, which are constantly transforming and changing. Second, this gift has defined a new stage of life for our 35 million people over sixty-five, a fact that is hard to ignore. We have given this new stage of life a name—*elderescence*. Elderescents are the benefactors of this longevity, with more time and space than previous generations in which to live and examine their lives. If this dramatic increase in the human life span continues, by 2030 we will have a population of 70 million persons over age sixty-five. The first Baby Boomers are approaching elderescence and they will not want to be treated as obsolete.

We studied the leap in human longevity from both historical and social perspectives. To determine that an evolutionary change has occurred or even that a change is in process takes decades to acknowledge. Given credence by ageist stereotyping and the consumer driven values of obsolescence, mandatory retirement for those sixty-five and older became the answer to the political/ economic crises of the early 1900s. This created a new population—*the retiree.* Retirement was the vehicle that separated and segregated this new population. Undoubtedly, few appreciated its long-range consequences on future generations and the eventual unfolding of a new human adventure. It provided a marker, though, for alerting us to a new stage of life. We believe the designation of *retiree* is a euphemism for someone who has reached this new stage of life.

Advances in medical technology and understanding have undoubtedly played an important role in increased longevity, as did institutionalized retirement. We suggest that the source of this gift of longevity is in the power of evolution; longevity "is inevitable; it is the logic of progress." (Roszak, *America the Wise)*

Blessed with an indomitable collective spirit, elderescents are moving into a position of greater prominence and power. Though, as Butler laments, "Older persons experience more stresses than any other group, and these stresses are often devastating." This will not deter their stories from being told, their gifts to society honored, and their voices heard. It has been our intention in this book to honor their dignity and courage to fight against ageism.

In speaking with elderscents and reading their personal accounts, we have identified four issues that demand attention: accepting the aging process, facing mortality, finding new meaning and purpose, and dealing with new challenges in relationships.

We have identified this stage of life as a transitional period, roughly spanning the years from sixty to ninety, often beginning with retirement. Although each person's story is unique, there is one universal experience—*Change.* The transition to a new stage of life may be characterized by new interests, pursuits, and values, as well as by an awareness of physical changes and a shift in consciousness. A shift in sense of self, though often not noted initially, will become central to how one manages this transition process from one stage to another. "Changes can engender exhilaration and be profoundly frightening. When it happens to who we think we are the fascination turns to fear." (Ram Dass)

Elderescents will face loss during this stage of life; it may be traumatic for some, leading to a sense of futility. The loss can refer to loss of professional identity, loss of youthful looks, loss of physical abilities, loss of relationships through death, and loss of the meaning and purpose that dominated the adulthood stage. The most paramount of these losses may be the loss of a future, which may be the 'crisis' of elderescence. While some may describe their new life as a "creative blossoming" or "finding new trust in oneself", "a filling up and spilling over", for others it is just plain "hell".

We view aging as a narcissistic injury and understand that it is often the first change noted in an elderescent's consciousness. This is a time when the paradoxes of life are more visible than ever. Elderescents describe being "alive and yet dying", "full of life's desire in the weakening body", experiencing "change and yet sameness", and "limitless imagination encased in a finite body." Physical changes cannot be denied. New research suggests, however, that mental decline in aging is not inevitable. Perhaps, as Deepak Chopra declares in *Ageless Body,*

Timeless Mind, it is even a myth. "Decline can be reversed . . . Awareness has the power to change aging . . . and retraining this creative potential is the mark of non aging."

Facing one's mortality rarely occurs with any concerted focus until elderescence, when approaching death cannot be denied. When friends and family members of similar age begin to die, life is understood concretely as finite. To give up the belief in the uniqueness of our individual selves can be daunting and devastating for many. In the words of these elderescents, however, the acceptance of one's mortality came after a life crisis. "I don't think I even blinked over mortality before my heart surgery." "After survival due to a medical miracle I moved beyond the follies of senior life into wisdom," and "the vision of the end of all things gave me the courage to say an unconditional yes to that which is . . ."

Profound changes in one's consciousness of death are unique to each individual. We understand through our interviews and through our readings that completing 'unfinished business' is essential, and desensitization to death facilitates one's acceptance of the reality of one's finitude with grace. Yet, many elderescents stressed the horror of prolonged life in a nursing home as the greatest fear. The acceptance of immortality can only be answered by faith regardless of how ones' beliefs are constructed.

Definite personality changes occur at this time. Through talking with and observing elderescents as well as reading social scientists' observations, we learned that elderescents become more dependent upon their partners as they age than during the adulthood phase of life. This dependency can precipitate a traumatic period of adjustment or one identified by a soft and lovely time of acceptance and intimacy.

Understanding the particular personality changes females and males experience at this stage is crucial for the happiness and even survival of many elderescent partnerships. In 1933 Jung first noted that men in later life become more passive and women become more assertive and aggressive. This finding has been corroborated and expanded by Gutmann. We have noted this as well in many of the elderescent couples we interviewed. If these normal shifts in psychological characteristics are not understood by the elderescents themselves, they can be misconstrued, endangering a marriage or a partnership.

Meaning is essential to living. Yet, it is easy to overlook a shift in one's sense of meaning during this aging process. At the turn of the twentieth century the established culture in this country informed the retiree that their lives were now meaningless. They were to rest, withdraw, and basically 'fade away.' By the 1950s some interest in orchestrating activities for elderscents emerged. The commercial 'sell' was to travel, move to retirement communities, or just have 'fun in the sun.' It was in the early 1950s that Jung declared that the meaning and tasks of old age must be appreciated as quite different. He wanted the elderescent to understand that what was meaningful in adulthood diminishes, fades, loses it's motivating power in old age.

By the 1980s a shift in consciousness about the value of this growing population had begun to occur. Elderescents themselves were seeking new meaning and purpose in new roles. But only recently has the fallacy that elderescence is simply a lessened or depleted adulthood been 'debunked.' As valid as the values of adulthood are, procreation, establishing a career and home, these will no longer be viable in the later stages of life. The elderescent must take a step back from the lives they have led in order to acknowledge and accept these external and internal changes.

Ego needs may diminish during this time of life as values shift and one's sense of what one needs evolves. Revisiting the question of meaning and purpose in life becomes an important task. The first step in this journey is, hopefully, an honest review of who one is now. What are the lasting features of one's personhood? What is the essence of being that has endured? Taking time for a life review, for self-examination, quiet reflection or meditation, or even a personal crisis, can awaken one to the changes occurring. Without an essential understanding of self, despair will cloud this aging process, diminishing the joy and satisfaction that can come with this new stage of life. An often repeated phrase— "understanding one's one and only self" is essential now.

Religion offers meaning for some, while for others meaning is found in less institutionalized forms of spirituality, in myths, in one's culture, through the creative process or through one's work. Analysis of human behavior as defined through psychology and psychoanalysis can provide a focus. Others find meaning living each day in the 'here and now.' 'Gero-transcendence' stresses the process of honoring transcendent experiences, opening to a oneness, to that which is greater than ourselves. This is seen as a natural outgrowth of letting go of the limitations of materialism and ego that come with age.

All of the above can provide structure and content for an individual's development of personal meaning. While each individual will find a unique sense of meaning, this will, however, be dependent upon internalized religious, cultural, social and family values.

Without meaning life becomes pointless. Suicide rates for elderescents are higher than for any group; twenty-five percent of suicides occur in people sixty-five and older. Jung projected the emergence of human longevity, but wisely suggested, "mankind would not reach the seventies and eighties if there was no meaning for the species to do so."

Life is empty without personal meaning. If this book offers nothing else, let it emphasize this fact: finding new meaning in this stage of life is a journey that has to be taken. Elderescents owe it to themselves and to future generations. In the words of Ralph Waldo Emerson, "A task is a life preserver. The purpose chosen will reflect the meaning of life that resides in the depths of our sense of our being."

In *The Stages of Life,* Jung offered guidance for the elderescent's journey through a process of reminiscing "in a spiraling or circular way that recognizes the unrealized desires of our soul . . . (that) elicits a creative, continuous process of becoming other than what we were, but at the same time, becoming more authentically what we are meant to be."

In this process we look at ourselves with a critical, honest eye; we think about dreams unfulfilled. We may resume the work left undone in adolescence, sorting out issues left unresolved, arriving at a new understanding of ourselves. If, in this last chance to know and accept who we are, we begin through introspection, to confront our shadows or darker selves, we may discover our most protected and denied aspects. This process may also enable us to confront our egocentric desires and find them not only meaningless now but actual blocks to emerging wisdom. If we can acknowledge our greed, our envy, our desire for popularity and material things, we can ask, "What more do we have to prove?"

This personal work releases us from egocentric drives and frees us to live unaffectedly. Perhaps we will even begin to enjoy what Chinen calls 'emancipated innocence', the enjoyment of intuition and creativity. This is a kind of spontaneity tempered by mature practicality. To feel whole, integrated, and affirmed by a deep sense of knowing who we are, leads to a genuine acceptance and joy in our authentic selves.

We feel we have just begun to understand how this new stage of life can develop, how this gift of time can be a source of wisdom for our world in crisis. We know that elderescents are providing invaluable services to their communities, demonstrating a unique creativity and skill that only those who have lived beyond adulthood can offer. Caring and nurturing the next generation is a central focus for many, an outer expression of an inner sense of abiding social consciousness. For others the focus is in a collective, creative force for change such as that found in the Conscious Aging movements.

Gutman attempted to answer the question whether longevity is a gift of nature, or medical technology. "We do not have elders because we have a human gift and modern capacity for keeping the weak alive; instead, we are human because we have elders." Is the desire to live longer the force behind increased longevity or is it humanity's need to have wise elderescents? We find Roszak's notion that longevity is the logic of progress compelling. Wisdom could be the benefactor of this evolutionary leap in longer life. "Evolution is the strife of a consciousness somnambulized in Matter to wake and be free and find and possess itself and all its possibilities to the very utmost and widest, the very best and highest." (Sri Aurobindo) In adulthood we are charged with procreating, becoming educated, creating a career, climbing the ladder of success. In elderescence we can take this extended time of living to search our internal worlds, our souls, for wisdom and meaning beyond the material and the physical realms.

We hope that this gift of longevity will provide the wisdom and vision necessary to help our fragmented world. Many elderescents envision the next evolutionary step as one that enables us to transcend the material realm and in so doing come to an understanding of humanity as one unified, evolving, and transforming entity. We will grow beyond the focus on money, beyond political and territorial battles, transcending ego drives, letting go of that which has fragmented our world, separating us from one another by the insanity of war. Chinen offers a promise that "in reclaiming wonder and delight in life" the elderescent assumes the role of mediator, communicating and linking the present world with the next, helping the young achieve a balance between the practical needs of society and revelations of a spiritual world.

Society must listen and elderescents must tell their stories; their struggles will be treated with respect and studied with great interest for what they will reveal about us all. President Kennedy's vision for our nation in 1963 was that, "It is not enough for a great nation to have added new years to life, our objective must be to have new life added to those years."

We end with the prophetic thoughts of G. Stanley Hall who eighty years ago noted with great foresight that "intelligent and well-conserved aging has very important social and anthropological functions in the modern world not hitherto utilized or even recognized. It is ours to complete the drama, to add a new story to the life of man, for as yet we do not know what full maturity really is. The world never so needed wisdom." (*Senescence*)

Appendix One

Hermeneutic-Phenomenology: An Alternative in Human Sciences Research

Because the field of psychology has sought validation for itself by grounding its tradition in science, the predominant mode of psychological research has been the experimental, behaviorist method. While this may have been appropriate for the fields of physics and mathematics, it does not address the true nature of human experience, which is not a fixed object to be tested and quantified but an ever-changing phenomenon. It seems unavoidable that research in a field must be done with a method that shares the qualities of that which one is observing and describing.

Can a method of research address human experience on its own terms, as a lived phenomenon? The hermeneutic-phenomenological method is an attempt to do this. Rollo May writes, "The phenomenologists hold that we must cut through the tendency in the West to believe we understand things if we only know their causes, and to find out and describe instead what the thing is as a phenomenon—the experience as it is given to us, in its 'giveness.'" (Kidd)

The underlying question for the phenomenologist is not why but what and how and by whom. The search is for understanding for its own sake. What is experience? How does it present itself? As Husserl states, "Back to the things themselves." (Kidd) This is a discovery-oriented approach, a method without preconceptions about where the research itself may lead. Experience is not an object to be controlled or predicted but a living, fluid phenomenon that one can only describe from within its lived state. This method does not seek to impose structure on experience but to observe and describe it as it is.

Experience is not seen as a neutral phenomenon but as a dynamic and meaningful one. How can there be psychological reality without meaning? The hermeneutic-phenomenological method seeks to reveal the underlying pre-reflective essence of experience that manifests as meaning on a reflective level. As Husserl has indicated, we can only describe experience as embedded in the stream of time and the life world. There is no subject separate from the object of experience; we are always in relationship to the life world in co-constituting our experience of it. This experience of engagement itself is integral to the practice of hermeneutics. The researcher must, in a sense, become one with the text, the author, and the question, she is exploring. As Dilthey writes, "Understanding is essentially a self-transposition or imaginative projection whereby the knower negates the temporal distance that separates him from his object and becomes contemporaneous with it." (Linge)

The practice of hermeneutics involves returning again and again to that which one is exploring. This movement is part of the ongoing hermeneutic circle in which one moves from the part, the particular, to the whole, and back again. In this movement, intuition is accessed, meaning is revealed, and the author, the interpreter, and the text are all opened to further understanding.

Appendix Two

The Experiential Method

The particular hermeneutic-phenomenological approach we have chosen to work with is the Experiential Method developed by James and Sunnie Kidd. This method is a way of investigating phenomena that echoes our ordinary way of understanding. It is a process of interplay between the reflexive and the reflective modes of knowing. The Experiential Method is immediate, intuitive, while the reflective is mediate, a "reliving of an already existing understanding of self and world . . . Heart is the reflexive, mind is the reflective." (Kidd) The Experiential Method is a creative process of understanding lived experience, of revealing meaning. It is an uncovering of the interpretation-of-meanings which are not immediately given. It is a relatedness backward and forward. For interpretation to begin, some understanding is already there, presuppositions of that which is to be, that which is beyond what was said. (Kidd)

The method consists of two preliminary steps followed by three essential movements. The first preliminary step is to clearly delineate the experience one wishes to explore and to compose a research question, expressing it in terms of a being, feeling, perceiving, doing, or having state. In this research we explore the experience of *being retired.* The question we have formed for this research is, "What is the Experience of Being Retired?"

The next preliminary step is to spontaneously write down one's own presuppositions about the experience one is exploring. In addition to these preliminary steps, the Experiential Method involves three additional movements that are the main body of the practice. These movements are followed in working with the research findings themselves: I. The identification of Experiential Expressions, those personal expressions of meaning that then become the Emergent Experiential Themes. 2. Affinitive grouping and Thematic Amplification, the expansion of meaning through intuition. 3. Reflective Synthesis, a returning to and reflecting upon the meaning of the whole through a synthesis of the personal and the universal.

After each participant's spontaneous response to the research question is gathered it is worked with individually. Within each Experiential Description, the phrases or sentences that emerge as particularly important or meaningful are identified as Experiential Expressions. These Experiential Expressions are then affinitively grouped as being expressions of particular themes of meaning. These are identified as Emergent Experiential Themes. The Experiential Expressions of each Emergent Theme are then affinitively grouped with the Experiential Expressions of that theme from the other participants. This leads to the amplification of each Emergent Theme, as the meaning of each theme is expanded through association between the Experiential Expressions from each participant's Experiential Description. In the final Reflective Synthesis, the meaning of the experience as a whole is synthesized by the researcher in a final statement. The Reflective Synthesis is then put into dialogue with the researcher's presuppositions as well as the literature review, resulting in a final conclusion section. With these three movements the Experiential Method becomes one of interplay between the participant's lived experience, the expression of this experience, and an expanding understanding of this experience for the participant and for the researcher, through intuition and reflection.

Bibliography

Achenbaum, W. Andrew. *Old Age in the New Land*. Baltimore: John Hopkins University Press, 1978.

Albright, Madeline. Interview by Cokie Roberts, ABC, January 2001.

American Association of Retired Persons, Bulletin, Jan 2003.

American Medical Association, Committee on Aging. *Retirement: A Medical Philosophy & Approach.* Chicago: AMA Press, 1972.

Annan, Kofi. "Who Will Pay?" in *AARP Modern Maturity,* January/February 2003.

Aristotle. "Rhetoric." in *Complete Works, Vol 2*, edited by Jonathan Barnes. Princeton: Princeton University Press, 1984.

Aristotle. *Politics of Aristotle*. Edited and translated by Ernest Barker, New York: Oxford Press, 1962.

Asawa, Ruth. "Profile." In *Women Turning 70*, edited by Cathleen Roundtree. San Francisco: Jossey-Bass Publishers, 1999.

Atchley, Robert, C. "Retirement & Leisure Participation: Continuity or Crisis?" *The Gerontologist* 2, (1971).

Atchley, Robert C. *The Sociology of Retirement.* Cambridge, MA: Schenkman, 1976.

Atchley, Robert C. *The Social Forces of Later Life: An Introduction to Social Gerontology.* 3rd ed. Belmont, CA: Wadsworth, 1991.

Atchley, Robert C. "Retirement as a Social Institution." *Annual Review of Sociology* 8, (1982).

Atchley, Robert. "Everyday Mysticism: Spiritual Development in Later Adulthood." *The Naropa Institute.* 1998. *<http://www.naropa.edu/atchley .html>* (20 May 1999*)*.

Autry, James A. and Stephen Mitchell. *Real Power: Business Lessons From the Tao Te Ching.* New York: Riverhead, 1998.

Azar, Beth. "Little evidence that old age causes work deterioration." *A.P.A, Monitor*, July 1998.

Bacall, Lauren. In "Whatever Happens." *Parade Magazine*, 18 May 1997.

Baker, Beth. "Open To Revelation, The Image of Older Men and Women Entering the Winter of their Lives is Changing." *Common Boundary,* September/October 1998.

Baker, Bruce and Jane Wheelwright. In *Jungian Analysis (Jungian stages),* edited by Murray Stein. LaSalle, Ill: Open Court, 1983.

Bateson, Margaret. *Composing A Life.* New York: Penguin, 1990.

Battin, Margaret. In "A Calculated Departure" by Barron Lerner. *Washington Post*, 2 March 2004.

Berman, Phillip. *The Courage to Grow Old.* New York: Ballantine Books, 1985.

Berman, P. and C. Goldman, *The Ageless Spirit.* New York: Ballantine Books, 1992.

Bernard, Kenneth. "The First Step to the Cemetery." *Newsweek*, February 1982.

Bertman, Stephen and Andrew Achenbaum. "Aging and Spiritual Empowerment: Stories of Oedipus and David." In *Aging and the Religious Dimension*, edited by L. Eugene Thomas and Susan A. Eisenhandler. Westport, Connecticut: Auburn House, 1994.

Bianchi, Eugene. *Aging as a Spiritual Journey.* New York: Crossroad, 1982.

Bisbee, Rick. "Letter." *The Phoenician*, Autumn, 1999.

Blake, Wm. "Auguries of Innocence." In *Portable Blake, edited by Alfred Kazil.* New York: Penguin, 1976.

Bohm, David. *Unfolding Meaning.* London: Routledge, 1985.

Bradford, Kenneth. "Can You Survive Your Retirement." *Harvard Business Review*, November, 1979.

Breytspraak, Linda. *The Development of Self in Later Life (Little Brown Series on Gerontology).* Boston: Little Brown, 1984.

Bridges, Bill. *Transitions: Making Sense of Life's Changes.* New York: Addison-Wesley Publishing,1980.

Burdett, Bob. "What Now?" *New York Times*, 9 February 2000 A12.

Butler, Robert. "Age-ism, Another Form of Bigotry." *Gerontologist* 9 (1969).

Butler, Robert. *Why Survive?* Baltimore: Johns Hopkins, 1975.

Butler, Samuel. *The Way of all Flesh.* New York: Modern Library, 1998.

Case, Bill. *Life Begins at Sixty.* New York: Stein and Day, 1986.

Campbell, Joseph. *The Power of Myth.* New York: Anchor Books, 1991.

Campbell, Joseph. *The Portable Jung.* New York: Viking Press, 1971.

Camus, Albert. In *The Adventure of Retirement*, by Guild A Fetridge. Promethean Press, 1994.

Canoles, Sister June. "The Nun's Story." In *Women Turning 60*, edited by Cathleen Roundtree. New York: Three Rivers Press, 1998.

Carp, Frances. *Retirement*. New York: Human Science Press, 1922.

Carroll, Lewis. *Complete Illustrated Alices' Adventures in Wonderland and Looking Through the Looking Glass*. New York: Random House, 1995.

Carter, Jimmy. *The Virtues of Aging*. New York: Ballantine Publishing Group, 1998.

Castenada, Carlos. *The Teachings of Don Juan: A Yacqui Way of Knowledge*, New York: Pocket Books, 1985.

Chinen, Allan. "Fairy Tales and the Spiritual Dimensions of Aging." In *Aging and the Religious Dimension,* edited by L.Eugene Thomas & Susan A. Eisenhandler. Westport, Connecticut: Auburn House, 1994.

Chinen, Allan. *In the Ever After*. Wilmette, Ill: Chiron Publications, 1994.

Chopra, Deepak, *Ageless Body, Timeless Mind.* New York: Harmony Books, 1993.

Cicero. In *Oriatones by Cicero*, edited by A.C. Clark. New York: Oxford University Press, 1918.

Clark, Margaret. "The Anthropology of Aging." Paper presented at the American Anthropological Association, Denver, 1966.

Clark, Margaret and B. Anderson. *Culture and Aging*. Springfield, Ill: Thomas, 1967.

Clark, Margaret. "The Anthropological View of Retirement." in *Retirement,* edited by Frances Carp. New York: Human Sciences Press, 1972.

Cohen, Dr. Gene. In "Longevity." *Washington Post Magazine,* 1 June 1997.

Cohen, Dr. Gene. In *Modern Maturity*, March 2000.

Confucius. In *Coming to Age: The Croning Years and Late-Life Transformation*, by Jane Pretat. Toronto: Inner City Books, 1994.

Costa, Dora L.*The Evolution of Retirement*. Chicago: University of Chicago Press, 1998

Crowley, Susan. "Auto Legend Back in Business: Iacoca." *Profile, AARP Bulletin*, February 1999.

Cronkite, Walter. In *World Federalist Newsletter*, 9 October 1999.

Cronkite, Walter. *A Reporter's Life*. New York: Ballantine Books, 1997.

Cuomo, Matilda. "The Gift of Mentoring." In *Women Turning 60*, edited by Cathleen Roundtree. New York: Three Rivers Press, 1998.

Cumming, Elaine and W. Henry. *Growing Old: The Process of Disengagement*. Chicago: University of Chicago Press, 1961.

Cutter, John. "Say Goodbye to the Office, Say Hello to Who Knows What." *New York Times,* 16 February 2000.

Cutter, John. "What Now?-Making Late-Course Adjustments to the Rest of their Lives." *New York Times,* 21 March 21 1999.

Dass, Ram. *Still Here: Embracing Aging, Changing, and Dying*. New York: Riverhead Books, 2000.

Dass, Ram. "A Stroke of Luck, A Conversation with Ram Dass." *Inquiring Mind* 17 No. 1 (Fall 2000).

Dass, Ram. "Conscious Aging." Audiocassette by Sounds True. Boulder, Colorado: Omega Institute, 1992.

Dass, Ram. "Conscious Aging." *Institute of Noetic Sciences Connections*, No. 5 (September 1993).

Davis, William. "The New School of Retirement." *Boston Globe,* 17 February 1999.

Deets, Horace. "Now Retirement Means New Opportunities." *AARP Perspectives*, *Modern Maturity*, January/February, 1999.

De Grazia, S. *Of Time, Work and Leisure*. New York: Vintage Books, 1962.

Delsen, Lei, and G. Redap-Mulvey. *Gradual Retirement in the OECD Countries*. Vermont: Dartmouth Publishers, 1996.

Dittmann, Melissa. "Fighting Ageism." *Monitor on Psychology*, May 2003.

Dostoevsky, Fyodor. *Crime and Punishment*. Banter Classics and Loveswept, 1984.

Downs, Hugh. Interviewed by Larry King, CNN, 2000

Drilling, Vern. *Closing Doors: Opening Worlds*. Minneapolis: Deaconess Press, 1993.

Dychtwald, Ken. In "Longevity." *Washington Post Magazine*, 1 June 1997.

Dychtwald, Ken and Joe Flower. *Age Wave*, Los Angeles: Jeremy Tarcher, 1989.

Eisler, Riane. "Twentieth-Century Renaissance Woman." In *Women Turning 60*, edited by Cathleen Roundtree. New York: Three Rivers Press, 1998.

Eisenhandler, Susan. "A Social Milieu for Spirituality in the Lives of Older Adults." In *Aging and the Religious Dimension,* edited by L. Eugene Thomas and Susan A Eisenhandler. Westport, CT: Auburn House, 1994.

Eliade, Mircea. *Birth and Rebirth: The Religious Meanings of Initiation in Human Culture*. New York: Harper and Bros., 1958.

Eliade, Mircea. *Rites and Symbols of Initiation, The Mysteries of Birth and Rebirth*. Spring Publishers, 1994.

Eliot, T. S. *Wasteland and Other Poems*. New York: Buccaneer Books, 1958.

Elwell, Margaret Coit. In *The Courage to Grow Old*, by Phillip Berman. New York: Ballantine Books, 1985.

Emerson, Ralph Waldo. *Essays and Poems*. Vermont: Charles E. Tuttle, 1995.

Erikson, Erik, Joan Erikson and Helen Kivinick. *Vital Involvement in Old Age*. New York & London: W.W. Norton & Co., 1986.

Erikson, Joan and Erik Erickson. *The Life Cycle Completed*, New York: W. W. Norton & Co., 1982.

Erikson, Joan & Erickson, Erik. *The Life Cycle Completed*. New York: W. W. Norton & Co., 1998.

Erickson, Erik. *Childhood and Society*. 2nd ed. New York: W. W. Norton, 1950.

Farleigh, Henry. "Diatribe." In *An Introduction to Social Gerontology,* by J. Quadagno. New York: McGraw-Hill, 1999.

Fetridge, Guild A. *The Adventure of Retirement*. Promethean Press, 1994.

Fischer, David Hackett. *Albion's Seed, Vol. 1*. New York, London: Oxford University Press, 1989.

Finneran, Riachar. *The Collected Poems of W.B. Yeats*. New York: Scribner, 1996.

Flaherty, Julie. "These Trips Fill Up Fast, No Matter the Destination." *New York Times*, 16 February 2000.

Fleck, Carole. "Retired Scientists: A Class act." *AARP,* June 2000.

Foley, Terence B. "The Hidden Disease." *Wall Street Journal*, 9 March 1998.

Fowler, J.W. *Becoming Adult, Becoming Christian: Adult Development*. San Francisco: Harper and Row, 1984.

Frankl, Viktor. *Man's Search for Meaning*. New York: Washington Square Press, 1959.

Freidan, Betty. *The Fountain of Age*. New York: Simon and Schuster, 1993.

Friedan, Betty, "Profile." In *Women Turning 70*, edited by Cathleen Roundtree. San Francisco: Jossey-Bass Publisher, 1999.

Freydburg, Margaret. *Growing Up in Old Age*. Massachusetts: Parnassus Imprints, 1998.

Fromm, Erich. *Escape from Freedom*. New York: Henry Holt, 1995.

Gadon, Elinor. "Profile." In *Women Turning 70*, edited by Cathleen Roundtree. San Francisco:Jossey-Bass Publishers, 1999.

Gallagher, Winifred. "Turning From the Workday World to the Spirit's Concerns." *New York Times,* 16 February 2000.

Gergen K. and M. Gergen "Lifeforce: Living Positively With Disease." *The Positive Aging Newsletter. <http:www.healthandage.com>* (6 December 2002).

Goldstein, Joseph. "The Practice of Impermanence." *Inquiring Mind*, 17, No. 1 (Fall 2000).

Goodall, Jane. "A Woman in the Wild." In *Women Turning 60*, edited by Cathleen Roundtree. New York: Three Rivers Press, 1998.

Gould, Roger. *Transformations: Growth & Change in Adult Life*. Boston: Little Brown, 1977.

Graebner, William. *A History of Retirement: The Meaning and Function of an American Institution, 1885–1978*. New Haven: Yale University Press, 1980.

Graham, Katharine. *Personal History.* New York: Vintage House, 1998.

Greenfield, L. J. and M.C. Proctor. "Attitudes toward Retirement, A Survey of the American Surgical Association." *Annual Surgical*, (3 September 2002).

Griffin, Richard B. "From Sacred to Secular: Memoir of a Midlife Transition Toward Freedom." In *Aging and the Religious Dimension,* edited by L. Eugene Thomas, and Susan A. Eisenhandler. Westport, CT: Auburn House, 1994.

Grinberg, David, "Age Bias with Older Workers." *AARP Bulletin*, February 2003. Guttman, David. "Aging Among the Highland Maya." *Journal of Personality and Social Psychology* 7 (1967).

Guttman, David. "The Cross-Cultural Perspective: Notes Toward a Comparative Psychology of Aging." In *Life Span Developmental Psychology: Normative Life Crises, edited by* James Birren & K.Warner Schaie. New York: Academic Press, 1977.

Guttman, David. *Reclaimed Powers*. Evanston: Northwestern University Press, 1994.

Hall, G. Stanley. *Senescence*. New York: Appleton & Co., 1922.

Hall, G. Stanley. *Adolescence: It's Psychology and It's Relation to Physiology & Anthropology.* New York: Appleton & Co, 1904.

Hareven, T and K. Adams. *Aging and Life Course Transitions: An Interdisciplinary Perspective.* New York: Guilford, 1982.

Harris, Virginia. "An American Quilter." In *Women Turning 60,* edited by Cathleen Roundtree. New York: Three Rivers Press, 1998.

Hartsen, Ann. In "The New Retirement: Redefining the Good Life After 65." *The Boston Globe Magazine,* 16 February 1997.

Havighurst, Robert, J. "Successful Aging." In *Processes of Aging: Social and Psychological Perspectives,* edited by Richard H. Williams, Clark Tibbits and Wilma Donohue. New York: Atherton, 1963.

Heikkinen, M. E. "Age-Related Variation in Recent Life Events Preceding Suicide." *Journal of Nervous Mental Disease*, (5 May, 1995).

Heilbrun, Carol G. *The Last Gift of Time: Life Beyond Sixty*, New York: Dial Press, 1997.

Heydt, Howard. In "Retired scientists: A Class Act," Fleck, Carole. *AARP Bulletin,* June 2000.

Hillman, James. *Force of Character*, New York: Ballantine Books, 2000.

Hirschfeld, Al., In "Broadway's biggest draw." *AARP Bulletin*, March 1999.

Holland, Gail Bernice. "Love Is In The Action, A Conversation with Laura Huxley." *Wisdom from Our Elders, Connections, Institute of Noetic Sciences*, September 1998.

Hope, Bob. "Retire, To What?" *Parade Magazine*, May 1997.

Hunnisett, Henry and Denise Lamaute. *Retirement Guide*. Vancouver: Self-Counsel Press, Inc, 1990.

Hubbel, J. "Staying Put." *New York Times,* 21 March 21 1999.

Hummel, A. "The Eastern View of Aging." Paper presented at the meeting of the Forum for Professionals and Executives, Washington DC, 28 November 1967.

Huyck, Margaret. In *Reclaimed Powers* by David Gutmann. Evanston: Northwestern University Press, 1994.

Jung, Carl. "The Stages of Life." In *The Portable Jung,* edited by J. Campbell. New York: Penguin, 1971.

Jung, Carl. *The Stages of Life: Collected Works, Vol 8.* Princeton: Princeton University Press, 1969.

Jung, Carl. *Archetypes and the Collective Unconscious,* Princeton: Princeton University Press, 1968.

Jung, Carl. *Memories, Dreams, Reflections.* New York: Vintage Books, 1989/1961.

Jung, Carl. *Modern Man in Search of a Soul.* New York: Harcourt, Brace and World, 1933.

Kaufman, Sharon R. *Ageless Self.* Madison: University of Wisconsin Press, 1986.

Kennedy, John F. In "Gerontological Social Work and the UN International Year of Older Persons," by Stanley Witkin. *Journal of National Association of Social Workers,* (November 1999).

Kelly, John, ed. *Activity and Aging.* Newbury Park, CA: Sage Publications, 1993.

Kidd, James and Sunnie Kidd. *Experiential Method.* New York: Peter Lang: 1990.

Kierkegaard, S. *The Concept of Dread.* New Jersey: Princeton University Press, 1844/1957.

Kierkegaard, S. In *Coming of Age: The Croning Years and Later Life Transformation,* by Jane Pretat. Toronto: Inner City Books.

Kierkegaard, S. In *The Meaning of Anxiety, by Rollo May.* New York: W.W. Norton & Co., 1977.

Kleeimeier, R. W., ed. *Aging and Leisure.* New York: Oxford University Press, 1961.

Kotre, John and Elizabeth Hall. *Seasons of Life.* Boston: Little Brown, 1990.

Kuhn, Maggie. "No Stone Unturned."Audio Tape. Sounds True, Omega Institute, May 1992.

L'Engle, Madeleine. "Profile." In *Women Turning 70,* edited by Cathleen Roundtree. San Francisco: Jossey-Bass Publishers, 1999.

LeGuin, Ursula, K. "The Space Crone." In *Women Turning 60.* New York: Three Rivers Press, 1998.

Levinson, Daniel. *The Season's of a Man's Life.* New York: Alfred Knopf, 1978.

Levinson, Daniel. *The Season's of a Woman's Life.* New York: Alfred Knopf, 1996.

Levin, J. and W. Levin. *Ageism.* Belmont, CA: Wadsworth, 1980.

Lewis, Robert. "Boomers to Reinvent Retirement." *AARP Bulletin,* 38, June 1998.

Lewis, Robert. "Older Workers Vow to Stay on the Job." *AARP Bulletin,* 40, October 1999.

Lifetime Living, 2 March 1953. In *A History of Retirement: The Meaning and Function of an American Institution, 1885–1978,* by William Graebner. New Haven: Yale University Press, 1980.

Lonkevich, Susan. "Artist Unleashed: Jon Sarkin." *The Pennsylvania Gazette,* 1997.

Maharishi. In *Opening to Inner Light,* by Ralph Metzner. Los Angeles: Jeremy Tarcher, 1986.

Mahler, Richard. "The Jubilados Experiment: A Sangha of Conscious Aging." *Inquiring Mind,* 17, No. 1 (Fall 2000).

Manheimer, Ronald. *Older American Almanac: A Reference Work on Seniors in the United States.* Gale Group, 1994.

Marsh, DeLoss L. *Retirement Careers: Combining the Best of Work and Leisure.* Charlotte, VT: Williamson, 1991.

Martinez, Elizabeth. "Profile." In *Women Turning 70,* edited by Cathleen Roundtree. San Francisco: Jossey-Bass Publishers, 1999.

Mather, Increase. In *Albion's Seed,* by David Hackett Fischer. New York: Oxford University Press, 1989.

Maxwell, Enola. "Profile." In *Women Turning 70,* edited by Cathleen Roundtree. San Francisco: Jossey-Bass Publishers, 1999.

McConnell, Adeline. "There is Life After 60." *Women's Day,* 1 November, 1999.

Mencken, H. L. In *The Evolution of Retirement,* by Dora Costa. Chicago: University of Chicago Press, 1998.

Metzner, Ralph. *Opening to Inner Light.* Los Angeles: Jeremy Tarcher, 1986.

McGrath, Charles. "Their Way." *New York Times,* 16 February 2000.

Milletti, Mario. *Voices of Experience: 1500 Retired People Talk About Retirement.* New York: Educational Research, Teachers Insurance Annuity Association-College Retirement Equities Fund. New York, 1984.

Minkler, Meredith. "Research on the Health Effects of Retirement. An uncertain Legacy." *Journal of Health and Social Behavior,* 22 (1981).

Moen, Phyllis. cited in "Age Wave," by Morley Safer. *CBS 60 Minutes,* 12 January 2003.

Morath, Inge. "Profile." In *Women Turning 70,* edited by Cathleen Roundtree. San Francisco: Jossey-Bass Publishers, 1999.

Morrison, Mary. *Let Evening Come: Reflections on Aging*. New York: Doubleday, 1998.

Mosedale, John. *The Retirement Journal*. New York: Crown Publishers, 1993.

Mosher, H. P. "On being a Professor Emeritus." *Annals of Otology, Rhinology and Laryngology*, 12 (Dec 1994).

Moss, Richard. *The I That Is We*. Berkeley, CA: Celestial Arts, 1981.

Moustakas, Charles. *Loneliness and Love*. Englewood Cliff, New Jersey: Prentice Hall, 1972.

Neugarten, Bernice, ed. *Middle Age and Aging: A Reader in Social Psychology*. Chicago: Chicago University Press, 1968.

Neugarten, Bernice. "Dynamics of Transition of Middle Age to Old Age." *Journal of Geriatric Psychiatry,* 4 (Fall 1970).

Nicholson, Trish. "Age bias 'alive and well.'" *AARP Bulletin*, May 2000.

Nicholson, Trish. "Boomers Discover Age Bias." *AARP Bulletin*, March 2003.

Nietzsche. In *Coming to Age: The Croning Years and Late-Life Transformation*, by Jane Pretat. Toronto: Inner City Books, 1994.

O'Connor, Colleen. "Cruising at 70." *The Dallas Morning News*, 11 August 1999.

O'Connor, Judge Sandra Day. In "State employees lose ground in age bias cases," by Trish Nicholson, *AARP Bulletin,* 41 No. 3, March 2000.

O'Connor, Judge Sandra Day. In "Courting History," by Laura Blumenfeld, *AARP Magazine*, July/August 2003.

O'Keefe, Georgia. In *Reclaimed Powers*, by David Gutmann. Evanston: Northwestern University Press, 1994.

Olitski, Jules. In *The Courage to Grow Old*, by Phillip Berman. New York: Ballantine Books, 1985.

Osler, Dr. William. In *A History of Retirement: The Meaning and Function of an American Institution, 1885–1978*, by William Graebner. New Haven: Yale University Press, 1980.

Pames, Herbert and Gilbert Nestel. "The Retirement Experience." In *Work & Retirement*, Cambridge, MA: MIT Press, 1981.

Pappano, Laura. "The New Retirement." *The Boston Globe Magazine,* 16 February 1997.

Payne, Barbara and Susan McFadden. "From Loneliness to Solitude: Religious and Spiritual Journeys in Late Life." In *Aging and the Religious Dimension*, edited by L. Eugene Thomas and Susan A. Eisenhandler. Westport, Connecticut: Auburn House, 1994.

"Pensions Memorandum, 1931." In *A History of Retirement: The Meaning and Function of an American Institution, 1885–1978,* by William Graebner. New Haven: Yale University Press, 1980.

Perel, Earl Jay. *The Case Against Socrates*. New York: Xlibris, 1998.

Perkins, Joe. "A New Plan: Work, Education, Diversity." *Modern Maturity*, July–August 1998.

Picasso, Pablo. In *Reclaimed Powers*, by David Gutmann. Evanston: Northwestern University Press, 1994.

Pretat, Jane. *Coming to Age: The Croning Years and Late-Life Transformation*. Toronto: Inner City Books, 1994.

Price, George. In *Reclaimed Powers*, by David Gutmann. Evanston: Northwestern University Press, 1994.

Proudly, Mabel Claire. In "Vounteers Honored for their Work by AARP." *AARP* Bulletin, April 2000.

Pruyser, Paul. In "Values, Psychosocial Development, and the Religious Dimension," by Eugene Thomas. In *Aging and The Religious Dimension*, edited by L. Eugene Thomas and Susan A. Eisenhandler. Westport, CT: Auburn, House,1994

Pulley, Brett. "Rolling Out the Gray Carpet." *New York Times,* 21 March, 1999.

Quadagno, Jill, & Street, Debra. *Aging and the 21st Century.* New York: St. Martin's Press, 1996.

Quadagno, J. "Aging and the Life Course." In *An Introduction to Social Gerontology*. New York: McGraw-Hill, 1999.

Quinn, Dr. Joseph. In "The New Retirement," by Laura Pappano. *The Boston Globe Magazine,* 16 February, 1997.

Rau, Santha Rama. In *A History of Retirement: The Meaning and Function of an American Institution, 1885–1978*, by William Graebner. New Haven: Yale University Press, 1980.

Remen, Rachel. *Kitchen Table Wisdom*. New York: Riverhead Books, 1996.

Riley, M. and J. Riley. "Age Integration and the Lives of Older People." *Gerontologist,* 34 (1994).

Rimer, Sara. "Late Bloomers." *New York Times,* 21 March 1999.

Rimer, Sara. "Enjoying the Ex-Presidency? Never Been Better." *New York Times*, 16 February 2000.

Rivers, Joan. *Bouncing Back*. New York: Harper Collins, 1997.

Roosevelt, Eleanor. "Letters to Eleanor Roosevelt.." The Franklin D. Roosevelt Library, 1934–1945.

Rose, Marcia. "Dharma Talk." Paper read at a three month Intensive Retreat, Insight Meditation Society, Barre, MA, November 2000.

Rosen, J. and D. Cuff. "Provide Provide." *New York Times,* 21 March 1999.

Roszak, Theodore. *America the Wise*. Boston: Houghton Mifflin, Co., 1998.

Roszak, Theodore. In "Boomers: America's 'true wealth?" by Elliot Carlson, *AARP Bulletin,* October 1999.

Roundtree, Cathleen. *Women Turning 60*. New York: Three Rivers Press, 1998.

Roundtree, Cathleen. *Women Turning 70*. San Francisco: Josse-Bass Publisher, 1999.

Rowe, John and Robert Kahn. *Successful Aging*. New York: Pantheon, 1998.

Rowe, John. "Six Myths about Aging." *Washington Post,* 20 July 1999.

Rybashi, John M., Paul A. Roodin and Wm. J. Hoyer. "Reports on Suicide and Alcoholism." In *Adult Development and Aging*. Brown and Benchmark, 1995.

Sack, K. "A New Life on Campus." *New York Times,* 21 March 1999.

Safer, Morley. "Age Wave." *CBS 60 Minutes*, 12 January 2003.

St. Augustine. In *Aging and the 21st Century,* edited by Jill Quadagno and Debra Street. New York: St Martin's Press, 1996.

Savishinsky, Joel. *Breaking the Watch-The Meaning of Retirement in America*. Ithaca, NY and London: Cornell University Press, 2000.

Schacter-Shalomi, Zalman. "Spiritual Eldering: A Conversation with Zalman Schacter-Shalomi." *Noetics Connection, no. 5 (* September, 1998).

Schacter, Zalman and Ronald Miller. *From Age-ing to Sage-ing: A Profound New Vision Of Growing Older*. New York: Warner Books, 1997.

Schmahl, Winfried. *Redefining the Process of Retirement: an International Perspective*. Berlin-Heidleberg: Springer-Verlag, 1989.

Scott-Maxwell, Florida. *The Measure of My Days*. New York: Penguin Books, 1979.

Shaver, Phillip and Carlin Rubenstein. *In Search for Intimacy.* New York: Delecorte Press, 1981.

Shaw, Bernard. In. *The Adventure of Retirement*, by Guild A. Fetridge. Promethean Press, 1994.

Sheehy, Gail. *Pathfinders*. New York: Norton, 1981.

Sheehy, Gail, *Passages*. New York: E. P. Dutton & Co., Inc., 1976.

Sheehy, Gail. *New Passages; Mapping Your Life Across Time*. New York: Ballantine Books, 1995.

Sherrid, Pamela, "Retired? Fine. Now get back to Work." *U.S. News & World Report,* 5 June 2000.

Simmons, L. W., *Role of the Aged in Primitive Society*. New Haven: Yale University Press, 1995.

Singer, June. "Profile." In *Women Turning 70*, edited by Cathleen Roundtree. San Francisco: Jossey-Bass Publishers, 1999.

Smith, Adam. "Wealth of Nations." In *Of Time, Work and Leisure*, by Sebastian DeGrazia. New York: Vintage Books, 1962.

Smith, Liz. "Profile." In *Women Turning 70*, edited by Cathleen Roundtree. San Francisco: Jossey-Bass Publisher, 1999.

Sri Auribindo. *The Synthesis of Yoga.* Pondicherry, India: Sri Aurobindo Ashram, 1964.

Staley, Eugene. "Creating an Industrial Civilization." *Report on the Corning Conference.* Corning, NY: American Council on Learned societies and the Corning Glass Works, 17–19 May 1951.

Stapleton, Maureen. "An Actress's Life." In *Women Turning 60*, edited by Cathleen Roundtree. New York: Three Rivers Press, 1998.

Steig, Wm. In *Reclaimed Powers*, by David Gutmann. Evanston: Northwestern University Press, 1994.

Stock, Robert. "Not An Age, but an Expanding State of Mind." *New York Times, 21* March 1999.

Storr, Anthony. *Solitude: a Return to the Self.* New York: Ballantine Books, 1988.

Streib, G. F. and C. J. Schneider, *Retirement in American Society.* Ithaca, NY: Cornell University Press, 1971.

Styron, Rose. "A Poetic Passion for Justice." In. *Women Turning 60*, edited by Cathleen Roundtree. New York: Three Rivers Press, 1998.

Szegedy-Maszak, M. "The Help Line." *New York Times,* 21 March 1999.

Taylor, Arthur. In *AARP Bulletin*, January 2000.

Taylor, Dr. Arthur. In "Tenure Gridlock: When Professors Choose Not to Retire," by Edward Wyatt. *New York Times,* 16 February 2000.

TIAA-CREF. "Born to Retire." *The Participant*, August 1996.

TIAA-CREF. "Lifestyles in Retirement." New York: Library Series, Corporate Publications.

The Organization for Economic Cooperation and Development. *The Transition from Work to Retirement.* Social Policy Studies, 1995.

Thomas, Eugene, L and Susan Eisenhandler, eds. *Aging and the Religious Dimension.* Westport, CT: Auburn House, 1994.

Tillich, Paul. "Loneliness and Solitude." In *The Anatomy of Loneliness*, edited by J. Hartog, J. R. Audy and Y. A. Cohen. New York: International Universities Press, 1980.

Tobin, Sheldon, Elise Fullmer and Gregory Smith. "Religiosity and Fear of Death in Non-Normative Aging." In *Aging and the Religious Dimension*, edited by L. Eugene Thomas and Susan A. Eisenhandler. Westport, CT: Auburn, House, 1994.

Toms, Michael. "Live Long; Contribute More." A conversation with Theodore Roszak, *New Dimensions*, July-August 1999.

Tornstam, Lars. "Gero-Transcendence: A Theoretical and Empirical Exploration." In *Aging and the Religious Dimension*, edited by L. Eugene Thomas and Susan A. Eisenhandler. Westport, CT: Auburn House, 1994.

Trafford, Abigail. *My Time.* New York: Basic Books, 2004.

Turner, Victor. *The Ritual Process: Structure and Anti-Structure*. Aldine Publishing, 1969.

U.S. Assistant Attorney in 1931. In *A History of Retirement: The Meaning and Function of an American Institution, 1885–1978*, by William Graebner. New Haven: Yale University Press, 1980.

Vaillant, George, *Adaptation to Life*. New York: Little Brown, 1977.

Vaillant, George. "A prescription for aging well." *Boston Globe*, 23 December 2001.

Van Gennep, Arnold. *The Rites of Passage*. Chicago: University of Chicago Press, 1960.

Viorst, Judith. *Grown-Up Marriage*. New York: The Free Press, 2003.

Wallace, Michael. "Jeanne Moreau." *CBS 60 Minutes*, 29 July 2001.

Walker, Joanna. ed. *Changing Concepts of Retirement*. Gower House, England, Vermont: Arena Ashgate Publishing Limited, 1996.

Welte, J.W. and A.L. Mirand. "Drinking, Problem Drinking and Life Stressors in the Elderly General Population." *Journal of Studies in Alcoholism*, (1), 56 (January 1995).

Weisman, Mary-Lou. "The History of Retirement, From Early Man to A.A.R.P." *New York Times*, 21 March 1999.

Whitbourne, Susan. *The Me I Know: A Study of Adult Identity*. New York, Springer-Verlag, 1986.

Whitman, Walt. *Complete Poetry and Selected Prose of Walt Whitman*. New York: Houghton Mifflin,1959.

Williamson, R., A. Rinehart and T. Blank. *Early Retirement: Promises & Pitfalls*. New York: Plenum Press, 1992.

Winkler, Milton. In "Retire? 'Boring', Says Village Man, 90," by Jacob Gershman. *Montgomery County MD Gazette*, 6 October 1999.

Winokur, L. A. "Road Warriors." *Wall Street Journal, Encore,* 9 March 1998.

Witkin, Stanley. "Gerontological Social Work and the UN International Year of Older Persons." *Journal of National Association of Social Workers, (*November 1999).

Woodman, Marion. "The Body's Wisdom." In *Women Turning 60*, edited by Cathleen Roundtree. New York: Three Rivers Press, 1998.

Yeats, W. B. In "The Body's Wisdom," by Woodman, Marion. In *Women Turning 60*, edited by Cathleen Roundtree. New York: Three Rivers Press, 1998.

Index

Author Biographies

Jane H. Thayer, Ph.D. a clinical psychologist in private practice closed her office in Washington, DC in 1995 and retired to Martha's Vineyard. She received licensing in Massachusetts in 1999 and resumed a small private practice. Before entering private practice in 1971, she interned at St. Elizabeth's Hospital in Washington, DC, was a staff psychologist at Alexandria Community Mental Health Center, a research psychologist at National Institutes of Mental Health in a Family Research project, consulted in therapy seminars at George Washington University and the University of Maryland and case management meetings at a local Vocational Rehabilitation Center and at The Kendall School for the Deaf in DC.

In 1972, she helped found the Gestalt Institute of Washington, DC, a training center for therapists. She was elected to several honorary societies: Chi Psi, Sigma Xi and was chosen for Who's Who of American Women in 1975.

Dr. Thayer has always been very committed to research. Her two-year definitive dissertation study compared schizophrenics' responsiveness with normal responsivity at St. Elizabeth's under a research internship, which was published in the *Journal of Abnormal Psychology, Vol. 77, April 1971.*

Dr. Thayer has an astute understanding of human interaction and an intensely inquisitive mind. She has become deeply absorbed in people's experiences of retirement and aging, observing and questioning others as well as reflecting introspectively on her own experiences. She is married and has three grown children and one grandson.

Peggy Thayer, Ph.D. brings to *Elderescence: The Gift of Longevity* her background as a practicing artist and a human sciences researcher. Her creative expression, her need to understand, and her value of the spiritual are all brought into play as she explores the experience of retirement and the issues of aging.

Dr. Thayer received her doctorate in East-West Psychology from the California Institute of Integral Studies in 1994 where she specialized in the spiritual aspects of creativity and phenomenological research methods. These studies provide her with a unique understanding of the transpersonal and cross-cultural implications of human experience.

For the last 20 years, she has participated in numerous one-woman and group art shows, receiving award recognition for her contemporary landscapes. Her publications include *A Reclusive Binge* in *Recovering*, July 1993, and *My Sister's Keeper*, book review, *AHP Perspective*, February 1994, *The Experience of Being Creative as a Spiritual Practice* Peter Lang, New York, 2003.

In addition to her creative pursuits, she has worked as a teacher of adults and children, as well as a research assistant on numerous projects in the human sciences, business, and literary fields. Currently, she is an adjunct faculty member of Akamai University where she has designed programs in Buddhist Studies and Creativity and Spirituality.